BEAUTIFUL UNBROKEN

BEAUTIFUL UNBROKEN

One Nurse's Life

Mary Jane Nealon

GRAYWOLF PRESS

This publication is made possible by funding provided in part by a grant from the Minnesota State Arts Board, through an appropriation by the Minnesota State Legislature, a grant from the National Endowment for the Arts, and private funders. Significant support has also been provided by Target; the McKnight Foundation; and other generous contributions from foundations, corporations, and individuals. To these organizations and individuals we offer our heartfelt thanks.

Published by Graywolf Press
250 Third Avenue North, Suite 600
Minneapolis, Minnesota 55401

www.graywolfpress.org

Published in the United States of America

ISBN 978-1-55597-590-6

4 6 8 9 7 5 3

Library of Congress Control Number: 2011923189

Cover design: Christa Schoenbrodt, Studio Haus

Cover photo: Iryna Ishchuk-Paltseva, *Death Autumn*

for Wendy Wilder Larsen
POET, MENTOR, AND FRIEND

Contents

Foreword

"THERE IS," WRITES THOMAS MERTON, "NO WILDERNESS so terrible, so beautiful, so arid and so fruitful as the wilderness of compassion." As a nurse, Mary Jane Nealon spent much of her life in just such a wilderness, and *Beautiful Unbroken* is her candid examination of that life. Nealon begins by recounting her coming-of-age in a tight-knit immigrant quarter of Jersey City, where she dreams of saving the world in the manner of Kateri Tekakwitha, Clara Barton, and Molly Pitcher. But even more than the examples of these women, it would be her struggle to free herself of ties to place and family, free herself of the burdens of her brother's fatal illness, which is quietly devastating her loved ones, that would most define Nealon's journey through the wild and spur her to work with the vulnerable and the suffering.

What begins as a desire to atone for leaving her brother's side in his final months becomes a clear commitment to her calling as she attends patient after patient during her own restless young adulthood in a country torn apart by the Vietnam War. That commitment eventually takes her to the heart of one of the most profound upheavals of the last decades of the twentieth century: the emergence of the AIDS epidemic. In Nealon's unflinching account of her work in a community of suffering and dying young men who are bewildered by what has befallen them, she simultaneously articulates the vastness of what she has witnessed and gives a particular face to the injustices of those years. At times, the membrane between self and society, self and other, seems almost indistinguishable, and always she discovers reciprocity in her work: "My story," she writes, "is about the gift I was given when I sat with the ordinary man, and later, with the ordinary woman. When I sat with someone who was ravaged on the surface, but who, despite stigma and cruelty, sat with her dignity and let me get close to her suffering."

Nealon's intimacy with suffering leads her to return to her aging parents, a return that would begin to redefine her way through the world: "I had begun my life with the dream of a few women. . . . Now I was middle-aged and I had finally fulfilled the dream. I wasn't a saint, but I had been blessed to meet so many who were suffering that the body had finally delivered all the lessons it held." When she then turns to poetry to help her shape the way forward and clarify her past, Nealon finds an exceptional voice—taut, frank, richly metaphoric— with which to tell her story: *Beautiful Unbroken* is about power of language as well as the power of compassion. But this memoir is above all an examination of a life, which is an examination of a conscience. And, after having traveled through the wilderness with Nealon, her readers may find themselves confronted with an essential question: What do we owe our fellow citizens, our society, our family, ourselves?

Jane Brox
Bakeless Prize Judge

BEAUTIFUL UNBROKEN

PART I
Wanting to Save Everyone

Where It Began

AS FAR BACK AS I CAN REMEMBER I WANTED TO BE A NURSE or a saint. I wanted to be heroic.

In Jersey City, our backyard was a small square that met the back-yards of our neighbors. The yards were as close as the houses. Our yard faced the backs of the houses on Fifth Street, and to our right, the backs of the houses on Erie Street. Everyone's clotheslines criss-crossed. Mr. Cleary's roses were big white and yellow bombs on the fence. Pearl Manupelli's potted plants and rusted rocking chair with the rooster cushion pressed in on the right. Alice lived to our left with her children and her wild barking dog, Lady. Three doors down from Alice lived the Polish man with the dog who looked just like Lassie. We called to the dog through the fence, "Lassie, come home!" In the center of our backyard, there was a dogwood tree, planted by my great-grandfather, Bartley Kelly. Once a year it rained velvety white petals in the yard.

One day my brother and I were playing catch in the backyard. My father was home, so it must have been a weekend. He had just come out to see what we were doing, or maybe to toss the ball around, but as he stepped from the back door we heard Lassie bark and then a scream that slit the leaves quivering in the tree. My father leapt the fences between us and the scream. My brother and I followed, but we were slow and afraid of Lady. By the time we got to the Polish man's yard, my father had cut him down from the shed where his wife had found him hanging. My father was trying to bring the man around, the wife was calling an ambulance, and Lassie was sitting back on her haunches, whining. Every few seconds the whines would escalate into a one-word bark. My brother held my hand, which he rarely did anymore, he was getting too big for that, but I was happy, because really I was holding *his* hand. I remember more people gathering at their fences and someone pulling us back over. I remember watching the superhero back of my father bent over the man. And the man's dark green janitorial pants. I noticed the bag of clothespins on the ground and the empty pulleys where the clothesline had been.

I remember wishing I was my father, jumping over the fence, saving the man. The man lived but his voice box was crushed and he would glare at my brother and me as we passed his front gate. We didn't think we could pet Lassie anymore because of the looks he gave us. He never forgave my father for saving him. It didn't matter. I didn't want to talk to him or pet his dog. I wanted to remember my father leaping in the air, the scream in front of him, and his quick flight over the wire fences.

The idea that I could be as heroic as my father grew in church, in the stories of my family, in our neighborhood full of immigrants. Our neighborhood was a kind of refugee camp: the Italians had mysterious basements they emerged from with homemade wine. *Rotgut,* my father called it, as Mr. Capezolli staggered across the street once a year with a gallon in each fist. The Polish women stood in clusters like birds around crumbled bread, colorful babushkas on bobbing heads. Juan, from Puerto Rico, opened a grocery store and refused to call it either a bodega or a *groceria,* a statement about his commitment to the new world. The lime-green sign read "John's Family Store." He stood outside in a long green apron, a sort of superhero cape, guarding the store from petty thefts. I would watch him from my bedroom window filling wood crates with plantains and mangoes and oranges each morning. In the apartments above the store there were first-generation Irish, like us, and Hungarians and Chinese. There were Russians in heavy coats. Our houses were tall brick tenements touching at the seams and in each one, a story of escape or poverty or hunger. All the old women knew the stories and they filtered down to us, playing in the street.

Our house was large and excessively decorated with ornaments from before the Great Depression. We had plush Persian carpets and gold-embossed wallpaper, but we also had inadequate coal heat that struggled to rise in rusted radiators. In the winter, frozen clothes from the clothesline stood in all the rooms. Pajamas going this way and that, a bra on the radiator, socks on the banister. We hovered near the radiators in winter, the clanking and knocking reassuring us that soon a little spurt of steam would come from the pressure gauge into the room. When I think about the house I think about turning a glass doorknob or dipping my finger into one of the holy water fonts. I think of the chaotic bird wallpaper in my bedroom and the heavy carved roses on dark furniture from the Roaring Twenties.

Jersey City was once the fifth-largest city in the United States, but our world was the twenty-two city blocks surrounding our Catholic house, and among the twenty-two blocks, nine Catholic schools or churches, and one synagogue. I was afraid of the rabbi and his wide black coat. When he would swoop down in greeting, I would run into our vestibule. He'd laugh and raise his hand in a wave. My mother was patient with my hysterics.

"I was afraid of Gypsies when I was growing up," she said.

"Is he a Gypsy?"

"No, he's a rabbi," she said.

In the early sixties, when I was six or seven, there was a Jewish man on Grove Street who was a tailor. I had yet to learn anything about the Holocaust or World War II; he was just another character in a neighborhood of characters. He made feather pillows. My brother and I would fling open his door sometimes and he would look up from his worktable and the feathers would go flying and he would curse in some language that we didn't know but we understood because he used the same bad gestures as the Italians. A few years later, after I had learned about the Holocaust in school, when I watched him bend over his table, his black vest and skullcap on a tilt, I would feel a spicy sadness in my throat, a burning up of shame.

I tried to eavesdrop on all the languages in our neighborhood: Polish, Italian, Spanish, and within the new words, English words buried in the accents, a brogue, a lilt. If you closed your eyes and sat on my front steps and listened to people talk, it could make your head spin. Each house had its own window coverings: white lace in the windows, thick brocade drapes, venetian blinds, bamboo shades, or curtains of multicolored beads. Each window was the country it came from, and behind each window, an old person sat, inspecting the new country.

We were also a neighborhood of sad stories. My grandmother sat on the stoop and gathered all the tragedies into her lap, repeated them as stories. By the time my mother repeated the stories to us my grandmother was dead, and most of the people in the stories were dead, so no one could correct my mother as she spun the tales (complete with moral lessons now) all around us on Fourth Street.

Somewhere in this childhood, which was not so different from anyone else's, I started to imagine that I was uniquely qualified to save the world. It started in the stories from the neighbors and moved into the stories in books. I made my plan for heroism in the whispers about the Irish Republican Army, in the closed fists of the old people dreaming of freedom. When I had crackers in Mary Donnelly's house or dropped a raffle ticket off at McLaughlin's, I would trace my fingers over their maps of a divided Ireland and imagine myself with a rifle and a loden coat capturing farms for the exiled neighbors. My wallpaper was a kind of metaphor for my secret thoughts, which were always about catastrophe and rescue. The paper was a faded blue with birds that were atrociously intertwined. No one could even tell if there were two or three birds in the picture that was repeated in a pattern the size of an adult fist. I would lie on my bed with my face in the picture and try to separate the wings and bird bodies, and it was an impossible torment.

My sister, Cathy, took on the burden of being good as the first child. She was darkly beautiful with reddish brown irises and a classic split between her front teeth. She had other marks of beauty: a widow's peak, a cleft chin. My sister was five years older than I was and my memory of her is that she was always somewhere else: at school, at my grandmother's house, at church. Our house was so big, sometimes she was only upstairs or downstairs but it seemed that she was very far away. In pictures of us from that time she stands quietly alongside me, her hands folded in front of her. I am hopping, or trying to pinch her leg, or in one, reaching out for her hand. She told me when we were older that she remembers being overwhelmed by sadness as a child. Being inexplicably sad.

I was pale with brittle teeth and lips that went bluish whenever I was scared, which I was, all the time. I tried to imagine my fear was what made me special; I was ripe for a visitation from Jesus or the Blessed Virgin. The miracle of my transformation would happen *because* I was delicate. I was supplicant, like the peasant children at Fátima, visited by Mary.

My mother said when my brother was born I was simply happy. He was as dark and beautiful as my sister. I tried to possess him. I held his hand and threw the ball to him. I wrapped him in a blanket and buried him in the sand. My sister floated above us, good as gold, getting high grades and causing no one a lick of trouble. I was distracted by schemes and little bits of trouble that I found around every corner. My mother was frustrated by my complaints and high screams, knots in my hair, notes home from the Sisters of Charity. She was frustrated by my glands, which were persistently swollen all around my neck through the winter for no reason that anyone could figure out, and she was tired of the blood tests that kept turning out OK.

My brother meanwhile was a good runner and a good reader as well. He had a laugh that was like smooth hay blowing this way and that way around the house. My father walked in and out in his policeman uniform except on Sunday, when he'd take us to church in his good suit. Some nights he worked an extra shift in the radio room, from 4:00 p.m. until midnight, and we'd get to call the police station to say good night. "Be careful what you say," my mother warned us. "We're being recorded." I would picture my father at the precinct on Seventh Street with the map of Jersey City lit up behind him and the tangible evidence of our call, a blinking red light on his phone.

The morning I found out Bobby Kennedy had been shot I stayed in bed, crying, and stared at the birds, then started picking at the paper with my colored pencil, then shoved the pencil into the wall until white plaster spilled out. Over the years, every time I was worried I would work the hole wider and wider until I started to fear a mouse would make its way through it while I was sleeping and land on my pillow. My father refused to fix it, as a lesson that one must live with mistakes. I tried to move my big wooden bed myself, away from the hole, then I stuffed things into it, socks and hair from my brush. It started to look like the tree hole in *To Kill a Mockingbird,* and from time to time I wished Boo Radley would appear behind my door.

Some days, my mother would pretend to be dead. If all attempts to get our attention had failed and we were being rowdy or pulling at one another she would just gasp and fall back onto the bed or slump in her chair. "Mom?" we asked. "Mommy?" Only when she knew we were appropriately stunned and worried would the pink in her cheeks come back. Then she would rise like Lazarus into the center of the room.

She also had a habit of warning us about doing things even as she did them. "Never put a knife into the English muffin stuck in the toaster," she would say, as she did it. "Don't ever do this, see, it is very dangerous, you could be electrocuted." Then she would add, for effect, "And if something happens to me don't touch me—I could still be electrified."

My father also found ways to scare us. As a cop he had seen every kind of accident, and he used them like parables to keep us in line. One night I was going to bed and I had a bobby pin in my hair. "Make sure you take that out," he said. "I had to go to a house one night where this little girl had a bobby pin go in her ear while she was sleeping, it went right through her eardrum." Some nights my mother would try to put little foam curlers in my hair that had to be held in place with bobby pins and I would be hysterical and crying about *the girl!* She would have no idea what I was talking about.

Another time we were with our father outside the Two Guys superstore on Route 440, and there were little horses on automatic rocking machines. We were begging for a nickel to ride them and my father said, "I saw a boy once who was riding one of those and got struck by lightning. Trust me, kids, you don't want to go on that." I developed a spastic colon to go with my swollen glands, and had a habit of pulling at my eyebrows when I was reading, and developed lots of other little nervous habits while I waited for horrific things to come from behind the twisted birds on the wall. My sister studied harder and made the honor roll. My brother charged out of the house laughing and everything happened to him. Almost everything I was afraid of would eventually happen to him.

My sister used to say that child abuse in our household meant that my father could read at the dinner table and we couldn't. Books moved in between the rooms, in between the walls. There were paperbacks with their pencil smell and heavy special-order books on all the bookshelves in all the rooms. We read cereal boxes at the table surreptitiously. We couldn't talk too much because, well, my father was reading. The first book that made me cry was *Orphans of the Wind*. I was in fourth grade and I remember sitting in the overstuffed flat gold chair, sliding on its shiny fabric. I remember two little boys on a warship and the way the evening light slid through the blinds. I remember my mother calling me to dinner just as I finished and how nothing that night, not even the salt in the crackers, could keep me from crying.

I idolized three women in my life: Clara Barton, Kateri Tekakwitha, and Molly Pitcher. I read their biographies more than once. They made the women I knew—my mother, my aunts, my neighbors— seem ordinary and boring. I didn't want to become someone who carried bags of vegetables home where I would slice them and drop them in water. I didn't want to wash clothes in big basins and hang them on clotheslines stretched from house to house. Kateri Tekakwitha, Indian saint. Clara Barton, founder of the American Red Cross. Molly Pitcher, who walked among Revolutionary War soldiers with water jugs and wiped their fevered brows. I didn't just read about them, I wanted to join them in their good deeds. My goodness was a nighttime secret. During the day I was stealing little things from my aunt's bedside table and my mother's wallet and hoarding them under my bed in a wood box belonging to my grandfather.

When I try to remember what it was about the pull of the life of caregiver and healer, all I can recall is the hard yellow of the Tekakwitha book, the way she knelt over the Indians suffering from smallpox, this "Lily of the Mohawks," the sketch of her, her face disfigured from milky pocks and ulcerations. I remember the last drawing in the book, after her death, when her skin was miraculously healed. I practiced her caring gestures under my sheet, pretending it was a teepee, laying a hand on an imaginary sufferer. The sufferer with parched and cracked lips surrounded by pox lesions, who smiled up at me, the only one able to take their pain away.

Saints were so familiar to me as a child they were like first cousins. I liked to kneel on the brown cushions in the pews and to take communion. I wanted to *be* a saint. I made a little altar on the marble table in my room and waited for my visitation, but sin was around every corner. I found myself telling little lies; they piled up. Was this the kind of girl who gets visited by an apparition? I had the desire sometimes to faint and just lie on the cold floor of the church while the parishioners walked over me. Instead I fidgeted and imagined Kateri Tekakwitha leaning over the Indians suffering from smallpox. She lifted burning sweetgrass over their blankets. In the background were the shadows of the black-clothed Jesuits she was prepared to die for.

My aunt Frances, who was a nurse, would walk in her crisp white uniform out of our house, carrying her cap from the Chinese laundry. I would hear the men on the corner: "Nurse, help, my heart is broken!" they'd call out. This was followed by whistles and laughter. She walked straight and fast until she appeared taller than all of them. The smack and twitch of their kisses hung in the air behind her.

It was in this neighborhood that once I started to see the impossibility of sainthood, the impossibility of reconciling my little thefts and disobediences with the miraculous, I paid more attention to my aunt. She took care of our neighbors' wounds and gave out advice and cough syrup, and it was among those days and in that luscious neighborhood that I began to think like a nurse, that I began to desire nursing. Among the other occasional fantasies I nurtured, like being an astronaut, being a nurse took over. I started, innocently enough, to begin my entire life.

My Brother's Accidents

MY FATHER WAS A SUBSCRIBER TO BEAUTY. HE ORDERED sets of special books: The Art of Russia, The History of Russia, The Art of China, The History of China. They came in heavy boxes and had black cloth covers and were in hard cases so they couldn't be destroyed by our handling them. He had sets about all the great wars and individual artists like van Gogh and Rembrandt. The books were lined up in the bookcase in chronological order. When I was in seventh grade my father got a slide carousel and a white screen like we had in school. Then he ordered a twenty-seven-volume set of The History of Painting that came over twenty-seven months. Each book had its own set of slides: Finnish Painting, Dutch Painting, Early Italian Renaissance. We would come home from school and he would set up the projector and talk about the slides.

"This here is Cassatt's *Woman Washing*" he'd say, then read the paragraph under the painting about the woman leaning over a washing basin. My brother and I would sit together on the white lumpy couch in the parlor and my father would bring all the beautiful paintings in the world into the room, where they would flash on his face and on the foot of the couch. My brother's skin was warm against my leg. Beauty was stacked up against all the accidents that might happen to us. Here, in this moment, we were safe together, our policeman standing guard, my brother's hair in my face. My father wanted to show us everything that was beautiful. This was his act of love. He ordered art and history in the mail as a gesture against the tragedy, as yet unnamed, that he knew waited for us all.

My brother had multiple once-in-a-lifetime accidents. When he was four years old, we were down at the Jersey shore and my father took him for a ride on a bicycle. The bike was a sky blue Schwinn with a flat backseat. They were riding by the Shark River inlet when suddenly the tires jammed. My father tried to pedal, but the back tire spokes had caught my brother's ankle. My father was frustrated with the pedal and pushed it harder. My brother couldn't make a noise because besides his little foot, his breath was caught too, and the world was a little *oh!* that wouldn't come out until his lungs would spasm and he'd finally make a noise.

It took 186 stitches inside and out to hold his tiny ankle together. Johnny came home after hours and hours in the ER. He had a plaster cast on his leg so that he would leave the dressing alone. He was set down delicately on the couch where we could all gather around him. He smiled at all of us because that was his nature. I had collected lightning bugs in a jar for him and he held them on his lap. My father was in the rocker behind us wearing a white terry cloth jacket and swimming trucks even though it was very, very late at night. I moved to my father's lap and I remember he felt clammy. All his muscles had let go and in some way I felt like he was sitting in *my* lap. The sad stories started for real in our house that night. My brother was only four and didn't seem to know yet that they would all be about him.

The next summer in the same house at the Jersey shore my aunt Frances was carrying a tray with a teapot and a coffeepot and lots of cups and saucers. Johnny came running through the room right into her. The boiling liquids poured down his little back, which was already sunburned from the beach, and it happened again, the hours he was gone at the hospital, the big white bandages that covered his back when he came home. He was on the couch again. I resumed my worrying, clutched my stomach, and picked at my eyebrows while my sister was doing anything she could to help my mother in the kitchen.

Cathy's sadness was the opposite of Johnny's exuberance. She moved among us seriously. I found her perfect quietude annoying, and it was only as an adult that I spoke to her about it. She explained how alone she had felt and I understood she had been as worried as I was. Her silence was a sad and tenuous solitude.

The summer I was twelve years old we couldn't play outside because there were riots. There were race riots all over the country that summer. I didn't really understand what was happening. Rioters were throwing rocks at open windows, so my father insisted we leave the lights out. We couldn't even turn the TV on. Two blocks away, on Grove Street, Molotov cocktails were thrown into windows to set houses on fire. My father had to work all the time. Our block was in his precinct, the station house just three blocks away on Seventh Street.

It was hot all summer. The air never moved through the windows open over the yard. One night I went into my brother's room and ran my fingers over the three-dimensional world map on his wall. I pretended that if I moved my fingers to the Rocky Mountains and held them there, I would be transported. The house smelled of smoke, and the sirens from the Pavonia Street fire station were wailing around the block.

During the day we played in the tiny backyard and stopped only for bologna sandwiches. When we played catch we would yell out who we were: *Mickey Mantle,* I'd say, and throw the ball. *Willie Mays,* my brother said and threw it back, and so on. We'd repeat the names and sometimes say the same name, there were no rules except we'd have to be someone other than we were. One day my brother tossed the ball and said, *Bobby Kennedy.* I dropped my glove and the ball rolled away. "What did you say?" I was enraged. The assassination was just weeks earlier. It felt sacrilegious to say his name. I could still see the black-and-white images from TV, the ones where he was looking up from the kitchen floor, a busboy kneeling over him. Men and women cried in the street. The morning before Bobby died, we imagined saying a rosary might save him. *OK . . . my brother said . . . he came to my side to pick up the baseball . . . Bobby . . . he tossed it . . . Drysdale.* I wanted to stay mad at him but I couldn't . . . *it's Don Drysdale,* I told him . . . and yelled out *Carl Yastrzemski* and threw it back at him. *Spell that!* he said. It was summer and we were tossing a ball under the dogwood and my mother was in the kitchen watching us. She called to us. My brother threw his arm around me. *Bobby Kennedy,* he whispered in my ear and shot past me through the screen door.

That summer I told my brother that I wanted to live in the country. My father had decided we should get away from the riots and took us to Cooperstown for the weekend. We had never been anywhere except the Jersey shore; we packed overnight bags and my father got us a book on the Baseball Hall of Fame so we wouldn't make imbeciles out of ourselves. My sister was already old enough to be working a summer job and couldn't go with us. My mother had a sleeveless blouse with pink and brown psychedelic designs and wore her hair in a loose clip. In the car we listened to the Mets game while my brother penciled stats in a notebook. My father still called them the Metropolitans. We listed our favorite players: Ron Swoboda, Ed Kranepool, Ron Hunt. I wore short culottes with polka dots and my brother had green khaki shorts, our legs side by side. We had no seat belts, so my father would take a corner fast and say, "Hold on, kids!" We'd slide together against one doorframe or another, my brother's shorts, my bare knees, and it was as if the excitement alone was pressing us together. At one point I said, "Ron Hunt is a fastball hitter and all this guy's giving him are fastballs!" I didn't know if this was true, but my father nodded and smiled in the mirror. It was my sounding sure that he liked.

Everything was perfect, the weather, the lake motel where we stayed. My father was calm, even when we were stuck behind an Amish man in a buggy. Our motel rooms faced a flat silver lake and there were individual porches with rocking chairs. After we checked in my father tossed *Bulfinch's Mythology* to me. "Read this, you'll like it," he said. And I did, there were gods and goddesses in the book. I was reading it to my brother in bed while my parents rocked, god and goddess to me then, on the little porch.

The next day, on our way home, the car broke down outside Pearl River, New York. We held our breath. My father would be angry. But he calmly walked to a pay phone and then said, "Well, kids, looks like we have to stay in a motel again, we might as well find one with a pool." My brother turned to look at me, and we saw my mother look at my father; she was as surprised and as happy as we were. That afternoon, in my navy and white dotted swiss bathing suit, I carried my brother on my back in a hotel pool. There were pine trees edging the pool area and everything had the scent of Christmas. When all the terrible things started to happen five years later I would torment myself by remembering everything I could about that weekend, most of all how my father kept surprising us, kept making us happier than we thought we could be. I would focus, too, on the pool lights, which were like little blue moons under the water, and my brother's legs wrapped around my waist in the deep end, his hands gently holding my shoulders.

The next day, driving home, I had my head in my brother's lap so I could stare up and see only treetops as the car sped along on the New York Thruway. "I need to live somewhere beautiful," I said to him. He looked down. He was ten years old, and he said, "You will, Mare, I know you will." And he pushed my hair back off my forehead with his left hand, a little boy who believed everything I said.

I had no sense of fear about the body, just a desire to cover it with a blanket or touch it or lie down alongside it. Sometimes I got to examine my brother's scars. All the accidents he'd had left their mark. Or we would be scrunched up together on the parlor couch and I would notice wax in his ear and because there was no boundary between us I would stick my finger in his ear and work it out. "You are sick," he'd tell me but let me do it nonetheless. I tried to mimic everything my aunt Frances did as a nurse. Sometimes I would put her white cap on my head and stare at myself in the mirror. I dressed up as a nurse on Halloween. In high school I joined the Future Nurses of America, which required taking temperatures and fixing fake broken arms. I reread the biographies of Clara Barton and Molly Pitcher. I started to see them differently, especially when I realized Molly had dropped her pitcher when her husband was shot in front of her, and had taken over manning the large gun. My new favorite illustration: Molly shoving gunpowder into a cannon, her husband bleeding at her feet and the other soldiers, parched or dying, behind her on the ground. Also behind her, a tattered flag waving in the wind.

In my last year of high school I asked my father about going to college. "You haven't studied for four years, you don't get to go to college without a scholarship. Nursing school is four hundred dollars a year, I'll pay for that," he said. We knew nothing about student loans and my sister did get scholarships for college. So I took a test in senior year and headed to nursing school just four blocks from our house. Tuition was low because in those days nursing students were used as labor in the hospital. We had two days of classes and three days of work. I liked the work. I already loved doing small things for the body: changing dresses, applying ostomy bags, doing bed baths. There was a ritual around the bed bath, using a thin blanket called a bedsheet. You were expected to wash people in quadrants, carefully placing the blanket to keep them warm as you moved from one area to another. I wore a blue seersucker uniform dress and white shoes. I carried little trays of supplies from one bedside to the next. Sometimes I massaged the feet of a patient after giving him or her pain medicine. I was my long-imagined version of Molly Pitcher. The instructors were impressed by my level of comfort with the body. On the weekend I might visit friends at the College of the Holy Cross or the University of Connecticut. I didn't mind that I had stayed behind.

I might have continued living in the fantasy of heroines, but in that first year of nursing school everything changed. My parents were celebrating their twenty-fifth wedding anniversary and they went to Bermuda for a week. They had never gone away without us before. My sister and I had friends over for parties where we blasted Pink Floyd and mixed vodka drinks. The whole week my brother stayed in his bedroom. I was angry at him, thinking he was opposed to our breaking rules and having fun. The day before my parents came home we cleaned and straightened the house.

The next morning, the car from the airport pulled up and my parents emerged, tan and beautiful. I yelled at my brother to help them with their suitcases, and he slumped to the stairs and burst into tears. He had been in excruciating pain all week but hadn't told anyone because he didn't want to ruin our parents' vacation. There was a lump. No. There was a grapefruit in his abdomen. It was hard and ripe. My parents dropped off their pastel gift bags and drove to the hospital, where he was admitted. I remember the vacancy of the day. The scent of ammonia in the clean bathrooms. My sister and I waited for them to bring him home. Would it be like before? He'd be propped on the couch with a bandage, smiling, apologizing? Instead, my father came home without my mother or my brother. Johnny had to have tests. I noticed that my father had paled under his tan.

The next day I was working on a unit adjacent to my brother's hospital room. I was measuring out medicines and reviewing their side effects with my instructor when our family doctor came down the hall and took me aside. He put his arm around me and said, "I don't know what this is, but it's bad, and your parents are going to need you." Then he left and I saw all the small lights from each of the doorways down the hall. I heard someone calling for help and someone else clanging a metal bedpan in the autoclave. My inadequate white shoes, my inadequate hands. What had I wished for? I did not want to be a nurse or a saint. I wanted to be a little girl in my brother's arms. I started pretending that day. I walked down the hall and reassured my mother. I reassured my brother, who was on his left side with his back to a green wall.

By Wednesday of that week my brother was at Memorial Sloan-Kettering Cancer Center in New York and after twelve hours in surgery we had a name for his tumor: hemangioperisarcoma. The doctors were hopeful but also said they'd only seen fifteen tumors like this before. We were smart enough not to ask about the other fourteen people.

My father paced the halls of the hospital. My mother crocheted an afghan. My brother hummed a song, causing us to relax, until he laughed and said he was singing the theme from *Brian's Song*. We were shocked at his hubris but laughed. *Brian's Song* was a popular movie about the death of Brian Piccolo, a football hero who'd had cancer. It was the way it would be from here on in. Johnny would be the one who would help us through everything.

Nursing School

THE NEXT COUPLE OF YEARS WERE A BLUR OF TRIPS TO THE hospital where my brother got chemotherapy and radiation, while I learned about the body and the body's mysteries in nursing school. Everything had a formal word: one-sided became unilateral, bruised became ecchymotic, swollen became edematous, and so on. There was a ceremony to everything, a certain way to make a bed, to give a bath. The first patient I gave a bed bath to was a middle-aged black man who had had surgery on an inguinal hernia. I folded the bath blanket over him and kept the bathwater in a big basin near his bed. I was timid, and he knew that. He took the washcloth from me, laid his hand over mine, and said, "You have to scrub. Don't be afraid to wash a patient like you would wash yourself." And then together we ran the washcloth vigorously over his face and neck, rinsed it, and dried him. He generously dismissed me and finished bathing himself. He taught me everything in that moment: that nursing was a kind of intimacy, and I needed to be confident in my approach to the body. I often thought of him when scrubbing a comatose patient. One time my nursing instructor said, "Take it easy, Nealon, you're not washing a floor!" But she smiled; she knew I wasn't afraid that I might hurt the body before me.

There were only forty-four students in my nursing class, all girls. I often took homework to the hospital in New York and tried to read anatomy or pharmacy chapters in the huge waiting room at the top of the escalators. Over the three years of classes we rotated through specialties: labor and delivery, psychiatry, pediatrics. In our psych rotation I went to a luxurious mental hospital in Summit, New Jersey. There were gardens and a Ping-Pong table. There were white

Adirondack chairs under elm trees. It was like an old TB sanatorium. The sad and confused patients shuffled in their Thorazine haze in and out of a cottage where they made things from clay and Popsicle sticks. I thought about Johnny's new baldness from his chemotherapy, or his mouth sores, and understood the sadness and confusion of the mentally ill patients. They opened up to me about their dark spirits. "You have a way with these people, Nealon," my instructor said. No, I *am* one of these people, I wanted to tell her.

My fantasy of nursing began to morph into the heavy chore of taking care of people. I applied dressings to a breast wound with crawling maggots. I was in the room during the birth of a two-headed stillborn baby. I saw a woman who'd been raped and had vertical knife slices up and down her arms. "It's not enough they raped me," she said. "They each had to leave a mark." I learned that many times there was nothing to say, that sometimes just not turning away from people was the best way to care for them.

After my brother finished his first year of chemotherapy and radiation, he had six months of good checkups and his hair grew back curly. He had a girlfriend. He lost weight and gained weight. He had mouth sores and vomited in the bed. He wrote poems about his fear and said things about Jesus that made me think he'd actually seen him one night. The second summer after he was diagnosed, he was in the ocean, bodysurfing. His scar was white under his tan and snaked down into his shorts, but he looked good. He looked healthier than he ever had. His shoulders had widened and he was strong in the water, giving himself over to the crashing waves. He swam behind me and pretended to be a shark. I was foolish enough to think everything was back to normal.

My mother said, years later, that she wished she'd given him the rest of that summer. Instead, when the doctors called and said there was a new tumor in his lung and he needed to come to New York immediately, she actually called him in from the water and told him and packed his bags for the ride to the city. There is a Celtic story in which angels play the harp backward for the dead. I felt the reversing notes and heard the music as he was taken away, waving from the backseat.

At the end of June 1976, I tried to hold on to the heroic fantasy that had sustained me most of my life. After all, I was a graduate nurse now, waiting for my license. Maybe I could find a way to save him. Maybe. But I also felt the need to flee. I needed to start the life I'd been waiting for. And anyway, he wouldn't really die. It wasn't possible he would die. I convinced myself that I needed to leave, to have the life in the country I'd always imagined, carrying a little bag of bandages and a stethoscope and taking care of others.

I randomly chose Virginia. Three weeks before graduation I was studying maps in the library at the nursing school and talking with my friend Nadine, who was also graduating. And also moving. She had decided on Charlottesville. We were friends, although at this time, not great friends; we just knew one another from school. I wanted to be like her for her confidence in her body and her little rituals for drinking tea. As we unrolled the map, she pointed to Charlottesville, showed me the blue and green areas on the map that meant mountains and lakes. I remembered tracing the three-dimensional maps in Johnny's bedroom, so when she said, Come with me, I believed, for just a moment, I might have a happy life.

When I moved away I left my brother. I also left ninety-four years of family. I left my grandfather and the Pennsylvania Railroad. I left the history of the way my grandfather died: tipped over in the front yard eating an orange. I left my First Communion dress, little bride dress for Jesus in May under the elm. I left our doorbell, our black telephone. I left wall sconces and dancing in the kitchen. I left my mother, doing the hornpipe, kicking up her heels, flinging the dish towel over her hair. I left all the baths I took with my brother and how we would make soap bubbles rise from the washcloths. But I also left his tumor. I left his suffering with the backdrop of the Colgate-Palmolive factory. I left the oily taste in the air and the suds that formed on our house's facade when it rained. "It's detergent in the air!" I once told my father. My brother said he wanted me to go. I thought if I repeated that to myself enough I might even come to believe it.

Before I moved, my father helped me buy a 1968 green Chevy Nova at Charlie Cacciatore's garage for eighteen hundred dollars and change. He thought it was a bad idea, moving in January with my brother so sick, but I had just gotten my nursing license and saved seven hundred dollars from working as a graduate nurse. Nadine was already living in Virginia, and my brother had a tube in his kidneys. He had had three surgeries for cancer that had spread to his lungs. He was stooped a little toward the side where they'd taken out a lobe of his lung. I felt, when I looked at him, like an elevator was falling in my chest. I couldn't breathe at the mere sight of him.

My father was missing so much from work from staying home to be with my brother he decided to take early retirement. My mother didn't argue one way or the other about my move. She was religious and was in a permanent state of puzzlement over what was happening to her son. She gave up candy for a Special Intention. She doubled her small contributions to the Maryknoll missions and said novenas, nine-day prayers. She continued to do all the other things she'd always done—cutting up oranges before dinner, folding towels so they faced the same way in the linen closet—but she seemed to be moving in sludge. She began each day crying over something that had nothing to do with us: the local bookmaker getting arrested, the butcher's dog getting hit by a car. We had never been close and now we grew even further apart; she thought everything I was planning was selfish. To her it was an abandonment of them all, pure and simple. I couldn't stay. I knew the inevitable outcome of the story: that Johnny would die. They carried their hope and faith from room to room in rosaries draped over bedposts, in scapulars around their necks.

The day I left it was snowing. My father packed my car. My mother and brother waved from the stoop. My sister was at work. I wore a dark green zip-up sweatshirt with a hood and blue jeans. My hair was in long braids and I had them tucked under a white beret. I was ecstatic to be going, but also filled with grief at leaving Johnny. None of us could bring ourselves to smile as I drove off. The block where I'd grown up faded in my rearview mirror. I would be back, I was sure of it, and so I spent very little time trying to remember the house or how my brother looked. Both would be gone within the year. I drove toward the turnpike with poems taped to the car's dashboard, playing John Prine music, heading for my life.

It snowed heavily all the way to Charlottesville, and took thirteen and a half hours to drive 360 miles. I sang all the lyrics to every song I could remember. Then I said the states and their capitals in alphabetical order. At some point I thought about the word I most wanted to forget: hemangioperisarcoma. I tried not to think about its scope or its size. I thought about the color of the scars that curved around both sides of Johnny's chest. I cataloged the many ways his kidney tube could be taped down, none of them sufficiently easing the painful tug he felt when he tried to shift in the bed.

I wanted to get there. I wanted to get there. Just before midnight I turned into the driveway of our apartment on Colonnade Drive. We were hoping to get a farmhouse now that I'd come. Nadine had waited up and we had pizza and wine. I unpacked almost nothing that night, just a picture of Johnny that I taped to the wall over my bed.

First Patients

MY FIRST PATIENT WAS A MAN NAMED ROY WHO'D HAD A stroke. Sixty-five days later his medical chart was into its third volume. Page after page of doctors' notes reflected his imminent death. Everyone was sure Roy would die, but he didn't. The medical teams were trying to figure out what to do. It had been sixty-five days since Roy had spoken or eaten on his own. His body seemed to have lengthened in the bed, grown more graceful. His delicate fingers picked the air like a woman picking lint from fine clothes. The doctors made rounds: bow ties and plaid shirts and khaki pants in an investigative circle around Roy. They were frustrated with this man who failed to proceed according to their plan. Roy couldn't go home unless he could eat and drink, and his family didn't want him in a nursing home. He had a temporary feeding tube that he tugged at and periodically dislodged. It was my first year as a nurse; to me these were small problems. What I fixated on was that Roy had lived.

When I bathed him, I would try to understand what he was thinking about by looking into his rheumy blue eyes. His eyes were small puddles, his lips cracked, his toenails long and curled. During the sixty-five days when everyone else had been waiting for Roy to die, I was getting to know him. Even before he came out of his coma, his body was strong and resisted being turned or positioned. I believed he wanted to drink water but no one knew whether his throat would work after so long. They worried that a few drops might accidentally fall into his lungs and cause pneumonia, a pneumonia that might kill him.

Eventually, the doctors decided that if Roy could be retrained to swallow he could go home. A speech therapist evaluated him and made a plan. She needed to train the nurses to do what she did, since she couldn't be there for every meal. We figured out whom among us would be trained in order to cover as many mealtimes as possible. The feeding tube would be a backup for days when no one with training was on shift. I was happy to do it, and even though Roy couldn't speak yet, he was communicating with an alphabet board, and his eyes were less watery. It seemed he was celebrating that we had finally accepted he would not die, something he'd known all along. I imagined that until we acknowledged his fight, it was a lonely place for him. The room seemed larger, and one morning, when I bathed him, we both caught ourselves looking at the painting on the wall behind me. It was of two boys in a rowboat under willow trees. I nodded to him and he nodded back. I was agreeing to help get him out of there.

During the year when I could not manage to be near my sick brother, I was helping an eighty-one-year-old farmer stay alive by mechanically swallowing with him. I held my hand over his throat and placed food in his mouth. Then I watched his eyes and together we began the swallow. I moved my hand up, then slightly out, then down, so together we were retraining his muscles to concentrate on the act of getting food and water down. Food was safer in many ways than water—liquids went down much too fast. If that happened, Roy couldn't cough, because his cough reflex was gone; instead he'd get a choking *look* on his face. I would lean him forward and suction him until his color returned to normal. Every day he got stronger, but each meal was a practice in patience, a meditation on nourishment. My back hurt from leaning forward, and I got behind with my other patients, but when Roy and I looked at an empty bowl on his tray, he'd squeeze my hand and tear up a little. I could see him in the boat in the painting on the wall facing his bed. I saw him back in his life, with his grandchildren, on the lake out past the turn on Barringer Road.

Nadine was working on labor and delivery, where she'd always wanted to be. We drove home together every night to a farmhouse we found after just one week of looking. Five boys from the university lived upstairs. They thought we were hippies because when we took our nursing uniforms off, we put on long cotton dresses and played reggae while we danced in the yard, or rolled down the hill, or made a spice cake with hash in it.

One night we went into town and I saw a guy with hair as long as mine, wearing a T-shirt that said *Buy Union Grapes and Lettuce* with a picture of Cesar Chavez. He was . . . *skipping* is the only word for it, down the street toward the same bar where we were heading. That's him, I said to Nadine, that's my type. Everyone is your type, Nadine said.

I danced with him that night and again the next night. His name was Rick and he was thirty years old. He lived with two guys from Jamaica who were seniors at UVA. Rick did manual labor at a picture-framing factory, and after a while I found out he couldn't read or write. He loved to brush my hair, though, and once spent three hours untangling the knots for me after we swam in the lake. He smoked hash and cuddled more than he made love, but he also helped me sand my bedroom floor and painted a border of horses up around the ceiling. We rented a piano. He bought me the sound track to *The Harder They Come.*

Roy started to say simple words because his throat was no longer as dry as a desert. He would say *good* and *pain* and *thanks,* but mostly he said *good.* I found myself speaking in single words, saying *good* more and more myself. Everyone around me seemed to be talking so much. Was it really necessary, all those words?

The winter was over and Roy had been in the hospital for months. During that time I also took care of a fifteen-year-old girl named Deborah. She had Wilson's disease, a hereditary condition that causes copper to build up in the blood and resulting in organ damage. Deborah's liver was failing, her skin was dark yellow, and her abdomen was bloated and tight. She was one of twelve children from *over the mountain*. I didn't know the name of her town, but her mother was the only one who ever visited, and many days Deborah was alone. We knew she would die, but the doctors couldn't make her a *no code*. The term *no code* is commonly used to describe letting someone die without interfering by putting her on machines to keep her alive should her heart stop or if she ceases breathing. Deborah couldn't be made a *no code* because she was on an experimental drug and part of a research study. Letting her die would affect the outcome of the study. When I bathed her I thought about my brother and wondered who was washing him. One day Deborah started to leak blood from her rectum, staining her underpants. She only had two pairs and I washed the blood out for her, but they weren't dry by the time she had stained the other pair. She started to fixate on the bloody marks and grabbed on to my hand. "Are they soiled?" she wanted to know. Sometimes I lied because I knew she didn't have a clean pair. I called her mother to ask her to bring her more. "That's all she's got," she said and hung up the phone. I went to Kmart one night and bought her ten pairs. "You cannot tell anyone," I told her. "It's unprofessional." It was our secret.

The day Deborah died I was standing at the foot of her bed, fixing her top sheet, when an explosion of blood flew from her rectum and covered the sheets. I called the doctors and grabbed the wheeled emergency cart, loaded with medications and breathing equipment. Deborah's eyes went wide and her skin started to shine with sweat but when the doctors came rushing in the room behind me, she stopped us all in our tracks by looking past us to the back wall, smiling, and calling out, "Jesus, you came!" Then she closed her eyes, and we all looked at one another. In an unspoken conspiracy we left her body unmolested. After a while we went and told her mother, who was smoking in the lounge. She asked to use the phone at the front desk to call her family. I led her to the phone and stretched the cord over to her. "Yeah, well, she died," her mother said, as flat as tin. I looked at the bun on the back of her head. I looked at her nicotine-stained fingers and her ragged pants. But nothing I saw in the woman on the phone allowed me to forgive her.

When I first moved to Virginia I established a pattern. I called my brother on Saturday mornings. The Saturday after Deborah died I called and though I hesitated at first, I eventually told him about what had happened. He didn't say anything for a second but then he said, "If I live I'm going to be a Jesuit and work in Bolivia." I went crazy, as though for a moment we believed he might actually live, and listed the reasons he should not be a Jesuit. Somehow we moved from that to Hemingway. He and I disagreed on something about Hemingway, I can't remember what, but seeing as my brother was always so good with facts, I backed down.

A week later I got a card in the mail with a ten-page paper he had written to finish the Hemingway argument. I remember the card. It had Porky Pig on the cover saying *Be A-lert, be A-lert,* and inside the words: *what this country needs is more lerts.* My brother wrote: "You should consider yourself lucky that I am writing you. I don't write for shit. If I sit up too long I get nauseous but if I lie down I get a headache. Someone has to straighten you out on your Hemingway problem so I figured it should be me. Love always, Les Brown and his Band of Renown."

I still have the card and the Hemingway paper. He had said I was lucky he was writing to me. When I reread those words so close to the end, I still consider myself lucky.

That September, Rick wanted to take me to Apple Day, a festival with fiddles and homemade applesauce in big vats over a true fire. That morning my mother called to tell me my brother was worse. Rick and

I hiked Crabtree Falls after the festival. The hills were a dramatic yellow and red, early changes for that part of the country. Rick laid me back against a rock and sang a little song and his curls fell over my face. "I love you." I said. It was the first time I ever said that to anyone other than family. There was a long time when he didn't say anything, and then he sat me up and held me and said, "You don't know what it means to love or you'd be with your brother."

His words. His words rose like the moon behind him. His words crackled and popped. His words flew up with the grackles over the field. What he said split my bones. Suddenly I knew everything about myself, and knew too, that no matter what I did then, I would regret these months in Virginia for the rest of my life. This man I loved, this hippie who couldn't read and who danced in circles, was the smartest person I knew.

I gave my two weeks' notice at work. I told Nadine and walked in the fields and told the blue flowers. Roy was supposed to go home on Saturday, so I didn't tell him I was leaving. He held his walker in front of him and took small steps to the desk, where he laid a hand over mine and said *good* and then *bye*. I wanted to cry but the other nurses were watching me.

The next morning I drove out Barringer Road to head back to New Jersey and I saw Roy in an ambulance in front of me, also going home. I saw his hand raised up in the window. I saw the blood-red leaves before me. I saw the hard road. For old times' sake, I put John Prine in the tape deck, and my life closed and opened like the hills and the space between them.

Unforgivable

REGRET BEGAN AS A LITTLE ROCK CHIP IN THE WINDSHIELD that on a cold morning cracked and grew larger and larger until I couldn't see the road anymore. My father was in his own car on the ice, drinking and not coming home. My mother was in an igloo cathedral with her blue rosaries frozen to her hands, and my sister, my poor sister, was trying to help us all and not disappoint anyone. To those of us sliding all over the road, blind or drunk, her task seemed the hardest. Even knowing my sister's burden, my regret found a way to resent her for the days she had to help my brother tie his shoes and tape down his kidney tube and hold the emesis basin under his chin.

Roy's body should've been Johnny's body, but it wasn't. Deborah's body was not my brother's body, so I might as well have been to a party that lasted almost a year. I had been in the wrong hospital. I had been at the wrong bedside. The sound track for my biggest mistake will always be the music from *The Harder They Come*. The landscape will always be a hill with blue flowers and ticks and my own half-naked body rolling down the grassy slope into the lake. What will happen to my body now that so much disappointment has taken up residence in my bones?

My parents had sold their house and moved into a place with an elevator since my brother couldn't manage stairs anymore. Ten minutes after I got to my parents' apartment, my father unlocked the door and my brother struggled in with his walker. I fell back against the cane chair. He looked like Christ on the cross, his bones visible through his shirt, his face sunken. But he smiled when he saw me. Oh, I knew I would pay for all the days I'd left him. When I was in Charlottesville I had purchased a flute on a whim. Rick taught me a few songs. Now, I gave Johnny a little lesson. He was so happy I felt like a criminal on parole. My mother frowned from the kitchen; my sister, when she came in from work, brought him baseball cards. I realized they had a little banter going, they had made a history without me. My family had been on a sinking ship and I went sneaking off on the only life raft; guilty, I came back to find them not drowned but hanging on to a single piece of wood. Oh, they didn't want me to die, but they'd just as soon I had stayed on my little raft.

Three days later my brother went into the hospital for the last time. When I remember Rick I think about the timeliness of what he said. I had the gift of those last few days at home. We had the flute lesson, and I had the sight of my brother's body in his own bed. Of his bright face when he walked in and saw me there.

I got a job working 3:00 to 11:00 p.m. in the cancer center where Johnny was being treated. I was working on the young adult medicine floor. My brother was on pediatrics even though he was now nineteen years old. Once a pediatric patient always a pediatric patient, the doctors told us. My job came with an apartment, so I got to live across the street from the center. I could see Johnny before work and after work, and sometimes I slept on a cot in his room. My father had started drinking at the Irish pub up the street, and my mother had stopped talking to me almost completely. She always had rosary beads in her hands. Sometimes when my father went drinking the nurses would call me because he was supposed to be staying with my brother and my brother wanted someone with him, but they wanted my mother to have her one night at home in bed. They conspired to keep my father's abandonment a secret.

I wondered whether I would be able to forgive my father for those nights when he left my brother, but then I remembered my own leaving and how big it was and how unforgivable it seemed now, and I found I loved my father even more for his failure. My mother's perfect way of being sad and praying and her *suffering* were the things that built my rage. We were all angry and circling each other like prisoners in an exercise yard. My sister slowly aligned herself with my mother and I slowly aligned myself with my father, and unwittingly we were already making a way for the family to exist without my brother, even though at the time it seemed unthinkable.

While I was working on the eleventh floor of the cancer center and my brother was dying on the fifth floor, I started wearing Laura Ashley dresses and leather Mary Jane shoes in all different colors. My hair was long, to my waist. I tied it with grosgrain ribbons or plaited it into braids. I started watching reruns of *The Waltons* and all my friends said, "Good night, Mary Jane girl," when they called me on the phone. I wanted the world to be an illuminated manuscript again. I wanted to carry a bucket of wildflowers and bake bread, but mostly I wanted all the death to get on a bus for the South and never come back. I had an idea about simplicity, about purity. I wanted to appear *untouched* to the world, as though my life was harmonious and not tied to my brother's poor body. As if I wasn't even remotely connected to the machines that surrounded him in the bed with cold metal side rails, to his skin, which was already settling in against his bones.

Instead it was December 6 and my brother clutched his chest and my mother and I were alone with him in the room. She looked out the window and he looked back at all his nineteen years through my face. He grabbed at his chest and shook and I yelled, "Somebody get the fucking morphine!" And someone did and my brother's struggle to breathe became a polite coma that lasted for five and a half hours and gave everyone a chance to hold his hand and say things we had been saying all along anyway only now he didn't have to look at us and feel sad or conflicted about how he should reply. At one point my mother said, "I knew it would be today. This is the day the twins died, and I asked them to help him." The twins were my older sisters who were born weighing less than four pounds, had lived a few days, and were buried in Holy Name Cemetery in 1951. When I was seven, my father said, as we drove past the cemetery gates, "You've got two sisters in there, Mare. I came down with them in little white coffins while your mother was still in the hospital." I pictured them then, one on each side of my brother, raising him off the bed.

Throughout the day, as we took turns sitting beside Johnny, I focused on his lovely right hand. The way his fingers had given up all struggle. Tapered, I would say. This hand. This hand I held outside grammar school on his first day of kindergarten when he wore a seersucker jacket and short blue pants. Hand in the bathtub, hand in the catcher's mitt. Hand exploding out from under a wave in Avon-by-the-Sea. Hand lifting a corsage to his girlfriend's dress on the day of the prom. My brother's hand filling out his NYU application. Hand receiving the scholarship a few months later. Hand that stayed in the air as I drove away from Fourth Street toward Virginia one year ago. Hand that just last night wavered about his forehead as he leaned forward and spit blood into the tiny mustard-colored basin. Hand that clutched and held on this morning and finally flattened, like this, on the bed where his body was going away.

The day my brother was lost on the beach I was five and a half years old. The day started out ordinary and calm. A parade of us walked the four blocks in Avon-by-the-Sea, holding our toys, the adults carrying chairs, a jug of juice, and straw bags with little embroidered sun hats. My aunt Frances had long legs and smelled of Coppertone. My mother was beautiful; she had a pink turban covering her black hair and a white see-through blouse over her bathing suit. My father would come down later with the car. We waved to him on the porch. Next to him my great-aunt Anne rocked on a cushioned wicker chair and peeked from under her white sun hat.

We played by the water and the adults sat just a little way up. After I had a small cup of apple juice to go with my sunburned shoulders my father came and we walked to the cove, or the low end, as everyone called it. There were no waves at the cove, which was sheltered by a long jetty, so children could safely play. It was a day of water and little rippling fun and sand. A day of getting wet and squealing and running away. Later in the day my mother realized my brother was missing and she asked me where I'd seen him last. I pointed to the water. That pointing. I failed to understand how the mistake of my pointing would grow like a storm cloud over the day. All the grown-ups walked and looked. The lifeguards joined in. More people asked me. I was wedded to where I pointed. I didn't know what had happened to my pail of seashells either.

All the other people on the beach packed up and went home to their barbecues. I was scratching in my swimsuit on a sea horse beach towel. I had little bluish fingertips and a shiver, but I didn't ask for anything. Then there were four long blasts over the town. It was the air raid siren, which meant either fire or car wreck or drowning. Volunteers came. Then there was a moment when my mother said defiantly, "I will not leave here without my son, do you understand me?" She planted her feet deep in the sand.

Aunt Frances took me with her on her search. We wound up close to the boardwalk because the tide was coming in and the beach was shrinking. Something compelled her to bend down and she looked under the boardwalk and she saw him sleeping in the shade. There was a wild excitement among my parents and the lifeguards. I can still see my brother, half covered with sand down one length of his little body, and can feel his chubby hand as he moved alongside me. As he resumed his place alongside me. We held hands the whole way home.

The thing I remembered most from that day was my mother's face in her pink turban and her refusal to leave my brother unfound. She never did leave her son, until all those years later, when he died and

was carried off by death's gray sea, which we first imagined, for a few
hours, had taken him when he was three.

The December night he died we went home to Jersey City on the
FDR Drive and it was cold and very gray, which was what one would
expect. I watched the back of my father's head as he made all the
right turns and measured the correct speeds and concentrated on the
road so we would get home in one piece, but truly, if he'd run us all
into the East River or the Holland Tunnel wall, that would've been
OK, too.

Once, when my brother and I played stickball, he jumped so high to
catch my wild throw, he landed on the fin of an old Cadillac. He was
impaled there. The sharklike car made a hole in his leg to the bone.
He was stoic for us, but I could see his careless flight in the circular
wound, how he tempted fate to lift him from the earth. I saw, in the
wound, his life, the tumor still undiscovered and higher up, so for
months afterward when he limped, we would think it was that freak
injury and we would remember that day, how stoic he'd been. We'd
remember his good humor, and the neighbors frantically holding him
in place against the fin. Some part of him loved the wound, loved the
unusualness of it. That night, driving home after he died, the fog and
black ice brought my brother back to me, as courageous and as un-
yielding as he was in the games we played day after day. Catch this, I
would say *(this wheeling, whirling world makes no will glad),* and throw
his life at him, like it was mine to give away.

PART II
Flying Nurse

Grief and Escape

All my life's bliss from thy dear life was given—
All my life's bliss is in the grave with thee.

—EMILY BRONTË

IN THE MONTHS AFTER MY BROTHER DIED, MY FAMILY BE-
came the quivering needle of a compass: my father disappeared north
into alcohol, my mother, south into prayer. My sister commuted toward the East River to work in a bank, and I went back to the cancer
center's hematology ward to care for other dying young boys, looking
for my brother. The narrow Hudson River that separated me from
my parents' apartment seemed as wide as the Atlantic Ocean. I didn't
want to go there; it wasn't our house, it wasn't what I remembered of
our home. The things that got left behind on Fourth Street when they
were moving in a hurry and trying to do the right thing now seemed
immeasurably valuable to me. Their actions seemed frivolous, careless, directed at me somehow. Didn't they know how much I would
need my Tressy doll with the button in her stomach that made her
hair grow? I was waking up angrier every time I remembered something that got left behind. My yearbooks? I would ask my mother.
My poster of Neil Young? Everything seemed irreplaceable because
everything was.

I wore innocent-looking dresses and piled my hair up like I was
living in the 1890s. I took a poetry class and had an affair with a
thirty-five-year-old man from Scotland. I went to work every day to
care for young boys who were dying and I was a good nurse, but nothing could make up for the frivolous ten months in Virginia. Nothing

could give me back those days when my brother was still alive in his bed and I was dancing like a fool so far away from him.

The year after my brother died, I tried to stay in the sphere of the living, but at the cancer hospital, young boys kept lining up in the hall. And I was so good with them. I could help them talk about their fears and I was such a comfort to the mothers, and even when I watched the fathers go back down the hall to the bar or their office I understood and made a bubble of understanding and forgiveness around my host families of death. Outside the hospital I dove into extravagance. I took poetry workshops at the 92nd Street Y, where I met strong women in their thirties and a handsome man I slept with and a tall black dancer who would become my first gay friend. I took private Latin disco lessons and wore wild floral dresses and went dancing at Cachaça, a Brazilian club, and met men from the Brazilian Central Bank. When I wasn't at the bedside of a dying boy I was exploding barefoot in the samba club with gray velvet couches. I called my parents once a week, on Sundays, and made excuses for staying in the city. One night the man from my poetry class called me in the middle of the night to talk about feeding me asparagus and making love in a Pakistani wedding tent. Language was a cave I was dancing into, a small light and arch of happiness. The boys who were dying hung all around me like bats.

Word circulated at the hospital that they were looking for a group of nurses and residents to go to Cambodia to work in a refugee camp. The International Rescue Committee was organizing, and Dr. Armstrong, who worked at the center, was recruiting the staff. I saw a way out. I signed up with a few other nurses who worked on my floor. We had to take culture and language lessons. Every Tuesday evening we met in a large conference room at Weill Cornell Medical

College, one block away from the hospital. We would go to Cambodia during the rainy season. There would be two shifts working twelve hours each and a van to share. I learned that you should never absently rub the head of a small child; to do so was to presume your soul was higher than the child's. We would wear green scrubs and get all appropriate vaccines. This would be my escape; this would also be my atonement.

One morning a few months before we were due to depart, the Vietnamese attacked the border where the camp was located. That night, an emergency meeting was called by the International Rescue Committee staff. Someone asked about getting to the airport, which was four hours away from the camp, if there was another assault. "Oh, if the Vietnamese attack again, *everyone* will be going to Bangkok," one of the facilitators said. The room filled with nervous laughter. I had visions of myself trying to jump into the back of a cart filled with refugees. I realized that I was terrified. Only about one-third of everyone there that night eventually went. I was changed forever. I never again touched the heads of small children without kneeling down in front of them; without understanding that their spiritual lives might be more advanced than mine, their souls might be lighter.

I started going to James Dean film festivals in Greenwich Village. The theater sold a ticket good for the entire day, and at about one in the afternoon they would show *Giant,* then *Rebel Without a Cause,* then *East of Eden.* People brought photos of James Dean and in between screenings everyone held up their picture like a Popsicle. Vendors outside the theater sold posters, postcards, and eight-by-ten glossy shots. Some of us carried brown leather wineskins in the shape of huge kidney beans hanging over our shoulders, a satchel with a spigot for our dreaming mouths. I had Mateus table white in mine. I'm not sure what other people had in theirs, but the festival got louder and more raucous as the day went on.

One Saturday, the festival started with Terrence Malick's *Badlands,* presumably for the way Martin Sheen resembles James Dean in *Rebel,* and also because one of the last lines of that movie is delivered by a deputy riding in the front of a police car who turns and looks at Sheen in the backseat and says to the other cop, "I'll kiss your ass, he don't look like James Dean." At this point, the theater went crazy, all of us whooping and hollering.

The thing is, I wasn't really a big James Dean fan, but I wanted the communion of the festival. It was a church without the morality. It was a Saturday in the Village, sipping tepid wine and wearing Jesus sandals and not thinking about my brother. One Saturday, in the middle of *Giant,* a boy about my age moved his hand to my knee and then, hesitantly, held my hand. That's all that happened. We held hands for the rest of that long film and at the end I let go so I could hold up my picture of James Dean. The picture was of Dean in a dance class with someone who looked like Eartha Kitt in the foreground. It was framed in a green mat. I went for the person in the next chair. For the comfort of something that started and ended and started over again in the dark.

In those days, there were two patients from Brooklyn I was taking care of. Young boys, in rooms next to each other. Their headboards met at the wall. Everything was the same but in reverse: as I went from one to the other, the suffering in one room was a mirror for the other. Tony was an eighteen-year-old baker in his family's bread bakery. Years later it became a famous place. The bakery was in *Moonstruck* with Nicolas Cage and when I saw the movie I could remember the feel of Tony's fevered skin. He had black curls and big dimples and leukemia. He didn't live long enough for his hair to fall out.

Jack was the other boy, nineteen, a student at Brooklyn College. He had testicular cancer that spread to his brain. He was bald from months and months of chemotherapy and radiation to the brain. He said to me once, "I was kind of relieved to find out it was in my fuckin' brain, you know? I was at this party with my friends and I started seeing weird lights and shit, and I thought, 'Jack, if your friends have passed you bad dope, they don't respect you no more.' At least it wasn't that." I remember when he said it I was handing him a milk shake and the frost dripped down the side of the glass and his hand overlapped my hand and he took the glass from me. The whole time I felt the glass might fall between us, but it didn't, and his hands, which were so pale they had a greenish tint, held on and then he raised one and patted me on the shoulder, as if to comfort me.

One night I took the bus down to Lafayette Street to read with Poets Against the Nuclear Threat at the Gallery for Social Change, and I ran into Tony's mother on the street. I was wearing a pale pink dress and pale pink ballet shoes. I felt unfaithful, dressed up, caring about the future. She grabbed my arm and wouldn't let go of me. "I don't want him to suffer," she said. "I can't let him die, but I don't want him to suffer." I stood there holding my little poems. I was just twenty-two years old but I told her that I would make sure he didn't suffer. I promised her. She stretched up to kiss me. She was only about four feet ten inches tall and round as a ball. "God bless you. God bless you," she said.

At the gallery, I started to cry when I read my poem "Agent Orange in Arkansas," and everyone thought I was passionate about the earth. A homeless man drank free wine in the back of the gallery. He stood up and yelled, "Fuckin' A, man! Fuckin' A!" I was ripped in two, cleanly, like a sheet of paper, pretending to care about big things, but all the while I was wondering how I would keep Tony from suffering. How could I keep his mother from losing him? How could I ever keep from breaking my promise to her?

In New York, a city of millions, I observed everyone. I carried a notebook everywhere and started saving stories, started imagining I knew everything about casual passersby. There were snippets of conversations I held on to and fleshed out, and in this way I tried to make a community large enough to disappear into. A man in a bar on Second Avenue came in one night and said to his friends, "I went hunting this weekend. I shot a deer nine fucking times! He moved, and I shot him again, he moved again, I shot him again!" I gave him a name, Mickey. I made him a batterer with an arrest record. I could see his T-shirts, bloodstained, torn, hanging on the shower curtain rod in his bathroom. In my imagination he would be transformed by a random act of kindness and move to Micronesia, where he would minister to the poor. Everyone who wasn't dying could be saved.

To others, I looked like someone who led a normal life, but occasionally in the grocery store or the library or on the bus I found myself looking at a handsome young man and then looking at his neck to see if there was swelling around his lymph nodes or if his skin had that now-familiar pallor. In my writing class at Columbia, there was a guy who wore leather, a bouncer at the Ramrod on West Street. When I read a poem one day, he said, in front of everyone, "I hate your mother-earth shit." I stared him down and didn't reply, and another boy passed me a note that said, "Don't hide, you're beautiful." I managed to ignore both of them because they weren't dying and so they didn't really matter to me.

Although I was surrounded by death I was oddly comforted by the boys whose bodies took on the shape of my brother's body. They all had the same cancer starvation, they all had delicate bones. And when they died, I washed their bodies and wrapped them in plastic, then cloth. Each tragedy reminded me that I was not alone in my tragedy. Each soul in each young body was a way to relive the moment when my brother's body opened and his soul widened in the room, then flew out from the corners of the window. I wanted to move on from the repetition of loss. I wanted to turn the compass on its side and run as far as possible from the quivering center, pointing this way and that way but never really stopping under the shatterproof glass. I was holding it in the center of my palm, trying to figure out which way to go.

Poetry and Escape

FOR YEARS AFTER JOHNNY DIED I CARRIED A LEATHER folder and a notebook. I would go to the Peacock Cafe in the Village and sit alone and write poem after poem about my brother's death. Eventually, I tried to remember every detail of Tony the baker, every detail of Jack. I used my fine-point pen and my journal to keep all the dying boys from completely disappearing.

In the spring of 1979 I took my third writing workshop in New York with Jean Valentine. She was a gentle woman who was able to make room around a poem and let people talk about it, but only if they could do so while continuing to respect where the poem had come from, to honor the impulse of making the poem.

During those days, I idolized Galway Kinnell, a young, handsome antiwar poet. Whenever Jean would say something positive about my work I would ask, "Do you think Galway would agree?" She knew, although I didn't yet, how dangerous an idol could be. She suggested I send him a few poems and ask to study with him. I sat at my desk with the stones from the yard in Virginia, with the stone of my brother in my lap, with the stones of Tony and Jack, and wrote something in a letter I sent to him. I don't know what I said, but I think I asked him for everything.

A few weeks later he called me. I remember I was looking out the window at the East River tugboats with the large Ms on them. He told me he was in New York and at a pay phone and was heading back to Hawaii. I could come to Hawaii of course, but what did I want exactly? He said it was expensive, very expensive to live there, but I heard nothing after the first *yes*. Before I'd even hung up the phone I was looking at everything I could sell: the few antiques I'd purchased in New York, the desk I bought in Virginia with the separate cabinets and little drawers with ivory roses for knobs. When I hung up I looked away from the river to the other window, I looked at the hospital's twenty stories and all the silhouettes of IV poles and patients in their beds. I paced the room like I was making the stations of the cross: I knew the window where the composer with pancreatic cancer was, his violin tucked under the bedcovers, and the room with the opera singer from Greece; the notes of a large song floated from his window to mine. I felt the stone that was my brother shift in my lap and almost fall out, except, of course, I still had to hold on to it, because in some ways this move was all about him.

Before I moved to Hawaii, I saved enough money to send my parents to Ireland for three weeks. My mother argued when I first tried to give them the gift of the trip, but my father just said, "Swell!" Their passport photos were the hopeless portraits of devastated refugees. They had been living for two years in the land without their son. This was the land of no reason not to drink alcohol and coffee and smoke cigarettes and be gray in heavy clothes. But now they were unexpectedly packing for a trip. They didn't realize they were packing for a trip so that I could leave in two months for Hawaii without guilt. They were folding and unfolding maps. And I was pretending I had done a good thing for once in my life.

They called from Ireland after three days. My father said, "Your mother is happy here, there is a crucifix and holy water in every room." It wouldn't be until years later that I understood what he was really saying was that faith had lumbered into the guesthouse disguised as a cow burdened with milk, and that they knelt on the earth and suckled all the nourishment they could. The Irish words they overheard in the café entered their hearts like the smells of their own childhoods. They reclaimed their own parents, then each other, then my brother appeared as a photo in their suitcase and for the first time in two years they could stand side by side and look at him in the picture without breaking into a million pieces of blue glass.

They met people along the road who didn't know their son had died and who looked at them expecting the happiness of people on vacation. My mother reclaimed lighter clothes, left the black and gray behind, and wore a pink wool sweater. After a while they found they could stand in a garden and not fall into the flowers. They found they could touch each other and all the recriminations were tied up with lavender as a sachet they put in their biggest drawer. The grief was still there, of course, but it was different in a country that was made to handle it. They could lay the grief at the foot of the mass graves of famine victims and it was appropriate there. They could carry it through the roofless churches with the hard marks of ogham slashed in vertical sentences. The ancient alphabet was my brother's spine in the bed. In the States their grief was out of place among new split-level homes and color TVs. But here the goats could carry it for them, up the rocky cliffs, across the bogs where some of them would drown. They could carry it over the rocks to the other side of the hill, the side facing the sun.

Their grief was a dolmen in the woods. A fox, golden and noble, circled it. They lifted the heaviest rock themselves and placed it on top and walked into the corn. In the cornfields everything was sweet. They tasted the way grief could shift in their mouths and came home and always said it was the best trip of their lives.

What is our responsibility when we stand alongside each other? At the elevator, at a bus stop, when ordering a bacon and tomato sandwich on rye, buying a movie ticket? Or not even alongside each other, but when we see one another from a car window? In the supermarket I watch a woman who has the same stance as my mother. The woman wears a pink cardigan with flower buttons; she buys a lottery ticket and some beef jerky and a packet of menthol cough drops. In my imagination, in the stories I am saving about strangers, the beef jerky and cough drops are for her husband, who is dying of lung cancer. She has no retirement because she never worked outside the home. The lottery ticket is for her, for a way to keep herself from a state-funded nursing home. They should've had children, but they were nearly thirty when they married and they just trusted it would happen. When it didn't by time she was thirty-five, she said a novena to the Sacred Heart, going to church every morning for nine mornings to sit in the pew near the back and imagine a black-haired girl with blue eyes.

I stood alongside her and felt a desire to lay my hand on her bony back. She looked at me, we smiled at each other. I saw she had a Band-Aid wrapped around her wedding band to keep it from slipping off her finger. "Good luck, Mrs. Colicchio," the clerk said, as she handed her the ticket. I pictured her husband at home, a pile of tissues next to his chair, waiting for the jerky and the cough drops. I pictured them sitting side by side on Saturday night, watching the balls fall in double and single digits out of the sphere with the forced air and rolling down the slide. Sometimes, it was too painful just to go to the deli to get a packet of cheese.

But what do I *owe* her?

Shortly after my brother's death, a friend of mine from high school went to Europe on a backpacking trip and felt sick when she came home. Her name was Donna, and she was as silky as a swan, her graceful neck ringed with a gold crucifix on a chain. She taught kindergarten and was an amateur photographer. Her favorite photos were of luscious bowls of fruit; she liked the fleshy truth of them, she liked the way a peach held light in its skin. While she was in Italy, she swallowed a bee that had flown into a Coke can. When she came back to Bayonne and suffered from extreme fatigue, she did wonder if somehow the bee had carried something into her. She always had circles under her eyes, it was part of her Mediterranean charm, but now they deepened to the color of baby bell mushrooms. The word I would use is sallow, she was sallow-complected. Her doctor didn't do any blood work, but said, "You crazy kids, gallivanting around Europe all summer, what do you expect? Take some vitamins."

Two months later, she was sunken into herself, except around her stomach, where air and something harder than air was growing and pushing her into the slight bulge of a high pregnancy. She went back to the doctor, who admitted her to a local hospital where she stayed, getting tests, for more than a week. The doctor mentioned Hodgkin's disease, and with the brazen confidence of someone very young, I advised her to sign out against medical advice and get her slides and films, which she did. I talked her into coming and staying with me and said she could see an oncologist at our cancer center. She did exactly that, and I called the most famous hematology oncologist of them all, a man who would eventually leave to become the first President Bush's personal physician. I called him and said, "You don't know me, but I take care of your patients on the eleventh floor and I need your help." He offered to come in before clinic hours since he was booked for so many weeks out.

The next morning Donna and I entered the darkened hallways of the clinic and walked toward a half-open door with a light behind it. The doctor was sitting at his desk. He took her slides and within minutes had a proclamation. I held Donna's forearm, she was cool and trembling. "I don't know what this is," he said, "but it isn't Hodgkin's and it isn't non-Hodgkin's. You need surgery to know for sure, but I don't think it's good news." He paused and leaned toward her. I tightened my hold on her arm, and we all just sat like that for a moment, for the beat of a heart, for the moment of a deep breath, and then he smiled and sat back and said, "I know who I'd want to do my surgery if I had to have this done," and he picked up the phone with the flourish of a rich and powerful man who was about to use his power for good. He said, "Don? I need a favor," as if he might have been asking to borrow the catamaran, but he was asking this man to save my friend's life, and we all felt it, we were sitting in a moment of hope in a steel room with slides of her bone marrow in little envelopes between us.

This is what we owe each other, I thought, to see the body alongside us and to try and save it from loneliness or from tumors that begin in the lung and end up in the liver. The old woman in the deli needs "Good luck, Mrs. Colicchio" like Donna needs a young, hotshot surgeon to come to her bedside and sprawl on the bottom of it and wink at her and make her feel beautiful despite a hard, encased lesion that is growing across the rise of her liver like algae on a rock at the sea, turning a smooth surface rough-hewn and unpolished and in the process, threatening her very existence. The disappointed faces of her kindergarten students when the substitute entered with her unambitious lesson plans in a plain gray folder floated over us in the room. In the darkroom where the surgeon held a portrait of Donna over a tray filled with chemicals. Would her image reappear? Would it fade?

It was about this time that I wrote the letter to Galway Kinnell, and while my poems were out there, flying in the air to Hawaii, Donna was discovering the particular stubbornness of her tumor, and the unexpected faithfulness of old friends like Eileen and new friends like Tom. Tom made her feel beautiful, even as she became bald, because she *was* beautiful bald, her long neck made for her skull. Tom had a girlfriend, but he still sat many nights after work at Donna's bedside, and brought her roses. She kept her sense of humor. One Saturday when Donna was home in Bayonne, we did mescaline and baked five loaves of bread. We wore roller skates in the kitchen and ribboned straw hats, like crazed Madelines in London.

I would say I abandoned Donna when I moved to Hawaii, but I wasn't the person closest to her. Eileen was with her, and her sister of course, and new friends like Tom. Everyone was drawn to her delicate disappearance, though it was anything but delicate for her. She held on to her life and wrapped it on her head in difficult knots of pure cotton cloths that she called scarves, until her bowed, wrapped countenance was all that was left of her.

Tom sent me two letters the year I lived in Hawaii. One described Donna's death and the crumbling stone of her immigrant parents. Of her father's daily treks to the cemetery, where he stood over a blank stone, unsure how to put her name there. If the name was carved in stone, there would be no getting her back. I imagined his thoughts in the cold November lines of mausoleums and overgrown weeds. Of her mother's silence, descended on the house and the remaining sister, and I knew this grief, I had seen it in our own home. This was the cyclone of parental love, grief in a black cloud carrying all the water in the world, spilling it in a thunder crack over the heads of the left behind.

What do we *owe* each other? The courage of skin, I believe, the hand on the forearm, the enthusiastic good-bye with its erratic wave. We owe more than we have. We owe more than we can bear.

When my parents came home from Ireland I was running out of time. Now I wanted to tell them about Hawaii, but they were so happy that I kept putting it off. One day in the car with my father, it felt like there was just enough time alone and just enough silence between us. I told him. He said he didn't blame me, I should do these things while I was young. He understood, he said, but my mother would be upset. I asked him to keep it a secret until the time I would leave was closer. I realize now I was asking him to take a big slice out of the newly found peace that had settled between them in Ireland, but at the time all I wanted was the conspiracy with him, the joy of knowing he understood my desire to go.

Two weeks later I told my mother, and her yelling and disgust came at me like I knew they would. She whipped out the *Ways Mary Jane Has Disappointed Me* folder and waved it at me, showed me how thick it was. My sister didn't even have a folder. She was a framed success story. I should have kept my father's loyalty secret in a red-stitched wallet in my pocket, but I didn't. I should have kept that

moment in the car sacred, the moment when he accepted me completely between us. Instead I used it to show her that he and I had a
separate love.

"Daddy understands, he supports me!" I shouted.

"How long has he known?" she asked. "Red?" She turned to him.
"Red? When did you know?"

She knew then. I did love him more. I had chosen him over her. I
scared her. She didn't like me. I didn't care, I had a blue suitcase with
a white belt around it and a thousand dollars in traveler's checks and
a contact at a hospital in Honolulu. I had my nursing license. I had a
plane ticket. Everything else had been sold. For the second time in my
life I was getting as far away as possible.

Years later, when I was in my early forties, my father and I were
in his car driving somewhere, and a Beatles' song came on the radio.

"Mare," my father said, "after you moved to Hawaii I used to play
this song over and over. It made me think of you."

The lyrics were a picket fence in the car. Were barbed:

> She's leaving home
> after living alone
> for so many years . . .

I had a glimpse of the hard slaps I had laid across their faces. Of
the cavernous mailboxes where the letters they hoped for were little
postcards with big writing to fill up the spaces. I had circled their
home on the map and gone as far away as I could. And it only complicated my love for them when I found out I was happier than I ever
thought I could be.

I was a puzzle even to myself. A friend told me I should spend some
time transitioning from New York to Hawaii. She sent me a brochure
about Esalen Institute at Big Sur. A note with the pamphlet said she was
treating me to a movement workshop. "You can leave some of your

grief behind and start anew in Hawaii," her note said. I decided to accept her gift. On my way to Hawaii, I stopped over in San Diego and rented a car. My dollars were rapidly disappearing. The drive up the coast was like a scene from *Charlie's Angels*. I was beautiful and in a little car taking the curves over the ocean, which was a grand ballroom for waves dressed in foam and fish. At one point while getting gas I asked the guy to check my oil. He was smiling at my white cotton dress and long hair. He said everything was great and sent me on my way. He hadn't put the oil cap back on, and when the radio was playing Procol Harum's "Salty Dog" a sudden spray of oil hit the windshield and the car pulled to the side and stalled. I managed to restart it long enough to drive it onto the narrow shoulder alongside rocks and little pink flowers. I was about forty miles from Esalen according to my map. It was Labor Day weekend. I got out and leaned on the car. Someone would have to save me. That was my only plan.

A few cars passed me. One actually slowed down and a bearded guy said, "Wow, car broke down, eh?" then waved as he drove off. I wasn't very aggressive about getting help. Finally, a man in a truck with a dog and a boy of eight or nine pulled over.

"Can you call a mechanic for me?" I asked.

"Well, I'm the only mechanic in town," he told me. "Let me go home and change my clothes and I'll come back."

The clothes he had on were raggedy, but he left and came back with different raggedy clothes and without the little boy. I was pacing. He pointed to a wooden building up the hill.

"I think you need to relax," he said. "Go on up there, give me about an hour."

At the top of the hill there was a craft gallery with an attached restaurant/bar. I sat on the deck that looked over the water and had a glass of white wine. The ocean was a blue parade, a circus of water rides and black stones. The gulls were acrobats. I found myself thinking of my brother and his poor body with its circular pressure sores and then of his crashing death, so when the waves hit, I saw him hit his chest, and I put down my wine and went back along the path to the road.

Under the hood the car looked brand new. He had cleaned every inch of it and replaced the oil. I would be on my way as soon as I paid him.

"How much?" I asked.

"Well, let's see," he said. "It's a holiday and I used four cans of cleaner and two quarts of oil and . . . twenty dollars?" I was relieved. I thought he'd charge me at least a hundred dollars. I gave him twenty-five. He looked like he'd just landed in a field of clover: dizzy and silly. He drove off. I drove off. The sea was a demon on the rocks below me, demanding I relive my brother's letting go. "Salty Dog." I had traveled far, but obviously not far enough.

Esalen was a social experiment. There was a gazebo and a cottage and a path to the water. Almost everyone was naked. Even the pool was nude and splashing. Picnic tables covered some skin but behind the salt and pepper shakers someone's breasts would be hanging down. I kept my white dress on but took my underwear off. I got the information for the movement workshop I wanted to take and went to the cafeteria for dinner where a man with a feather in his hair scooped beans into a little pita shell on my plate. I focused on his left nipple. I avoided his eyes, along with everything else he had on display. The woman in charge told me I either had to help serve or help clean up. Clean up, I told her, and sat with my beans, facing the water.

Before we washed the dishes and stacked them for the next day, we made a circle of almost nakedness and held hands and said a meditation about work. I was eager for my cabin and the quilt over the bed. I was eager for the sounds of the woodpecker nesting in the beams. I was in a dangerous place. My tension was leaving, I was almost wanting to be naked, too.

The first day of the workshop was about candles and chanting and sweeping our arms into big circles. My body felt loose and soft. There were men with long hair and women with shaved heads. I found that

I loved my feet more than anything else in our exercise of finding a part of ourselves we loved.

That night I positioned myself in the kitchen next to the man with the feather so when we had to hold hands before the mess of the dishes I got to hold his. He was in his twenties like me.

"What's your name?" I asked him.

"Joseph," he said.

We scrubbed pots. Someone sang an Indian song. I went back to my cabin and listened to the crash of the ocean below. A thin black spider ran across my foot.

On the third day of the workshop I got kicked out because I wouldn't scream.

"I don't need to scream," I said.

"You have to scream," the leader of the group said.

"It's not a primal scream workshop. It's a movement workshop."

"We are moving toward the primal scream," I was told.

"No." I'd heard people screaming in hospitals, I thought. I wouldn't scream in a village with a gazebo and naked dancers.

I was told I had to leave. The people who wanted to scream were looking at me and frowning. Their movement work was betraying them. Their muscles were angry, their screams were failing them.

I was happy that I'd been kicked out. It was only 11:00 a.m. and I went walking on a path in the woods. I had on a white sundress that crossed over my back and on my feet I wore flat cloth Chinese slippers. I was thinking of fuchsia blossoms. I tried to empty my mind of everything but fuchsia blossoms. It worked. I floated on the scent of pine needles and honeysuckle. Joseph stepped around the curve of road. He had a walking stick with Celtic circles carved into it.

"What happened?" he asked.

"I got kicked out of the primal scream workshop because I wouldn't scream."

He laughed.

"Just as well," he said. "I wanted to do a spiritual reading for you."

We walked to his cabin. I realized I hadn't really spoken to anyone for almost four days except for the conversation in the workshop and the night I asked him his name. The woods opened up to a cabin just like mine. I took my shoes off because he did. He asked me to lie on the floor and I did. He asked me to let him cover me with blankets and I did. The blankets were as thin as leaves and he laid them over me, covering all of me, even my face.

"I need you to close your eyes and go inside," he said. Then more blankets. I could still breathe, but there were about thirty layers on top of me. He started to peel them back and told me all about myself.

"You love the earth," he said first, and then other things no one could argue with: "water is your element" and "friends matter to you." But when he said, "You have suffered a large grief, the loss of a male in your life, and you are going to cross the ocean," my eyes shot open under the blankets. "No, stay *inside*," he said. I can't explain how he knew I'd opened my eyes, but I went back inside and crossed the sea to my new home, where the magnificent volcanic cliffs and their mossy edges might just be big enough to hold the edge of my loss.

Finally the last blanket was uncovered. He tucked me in. "Stay as long as you'd like," he said, and kissed me on the forehead. I fell asleep for about twenty minutes and dreamed of white horses pounding down the mountain in mist. When I woke, I went outside and Joseph had stuffed fuchsia blossoms in my shoes. I reentered the mystery of the church. My life was a parable, a miracle. I had a slice of bread, it was the holy host. The saints swayed in my closet and the cabin's walls fell away. I flew over rock edges and held hands that night with all the strangers in the kitchen and stared at Joseph while I concentrated on cleanliness and silverware. Big Sur was the rumor of a new world, a blossom, a feather in sun-bleached hair, a naked man with thirty felt blankets.

There Is No Escape

I GOT OFF THE PLANE IN HONOLULU AND REALIZED RIGHT away I was in trouble. I had imagined arriving in a village with huts where I would find a sign that said Rooms for Let. I didn't know it would be such a large city, and then of course, I thought, *Hawaii Five-0!* I should've remembered. I took my suitcase and turned from the exit door of the airport and headed straight for the airport lounge, where I ordered a piña colada and bought a newspaper. I met a guy waiting for his friends, who were also nurses, and they offered to let me live with them. The guy was compact, a kind of walking tour guide with a tan body and a Hawaiian shirt, even though just three weeks earlier he'd moved here from Massachusetts. I moved in with them that day.

That was the kind of life I was leading, just going along, taking all kinds of chances. I learned the bus routes and got to the university, where I was taking Galway's writing classes and his translation class. I got a job with a local nursing agency and started sleeping with the guy from the airport. He had a name, Raymond. But it doesn't matter that he had a name. I was either escaping into bodies that were sick or escaping into bodies that were well. I was fascinated by the body and its functions and still wondered how my brother's body had failed him. I was falling mindlessly into everything in those days. I fell into the ocean where the yellow fish and their bubbles made an explosion of soft air around my body. I fell into the windward rain and the orchids and the mynah birds.

There were a few months when I was sitting in Galway's class and I was blinded by my idol cloud. But soon I noticed how scantily clothed the female students were, and how he flirted, and I gave up my false idol and focused on the poetry and what I could learn from him, and that freed me. After three months, I left Ray and got my own apartment on Kaneohe Bay and would lie on the roof at night and try to make out the image of my brother in the stars. During this time I called my parents every Sunday, but only on Sunday. There was nothing generous or spontaneous in my contact with them. My calls felt like a chore and they knew that, I think, because the line was often silent in between moments while we thought of things to tell each other about our lives.

The comfort of patients was that they were the same everywhere. In Hawaii, the ocean was mint green and as clear as glass. The air smelled sweet from all the flowers around my house, but the patients on the oncology ward had the same frailties as the patients in New York. I rubbed the same rib shapes through tender backs. I wore my white stockings on the night shift. I lived in Kaneohe, on the windward side, and settled into a life of afternoon rain and insects buzzing over makeshift streams in the road. I settled into mornings sleeping on the beach and snorkeled among yellow fish that slipped between my thighs.

One night I got an admission, a man who the doctors thought might have pancreatic cancer. They put a chest tube in between his ribs, alongside his collapsed lung. His wife described a weight loss of sixty pounds in a few months and watery diarrhea. He had bloating and upper back pain. The doctors imagined it was cancer that had spread to his lung that caused the collapse. On x-rays, everything was cloudy and white. They put in a central line, a catheter in a large blood vessel in his chest, so he could get nutrition even if he couldn't eat. He was scheduled for tests in the morning, and I was in the room with a nurse's aide named David. I was at the sink explaining the CAT scans to the patient, and why they were necessary, when he coughed. I could see something hanging from his mouth. I asked the nurse's aide, "David, can you wipe his mouth for me?" I saw David lean over the man and take a swipe with a Kleenex, then I saw him go back over the man's mouth, and again, until he held up something eight inches long and writhing. It was a worm as thick as my thumb. I turned to the sink and vomited, then quickly apologized to the patient, who was pale and shaking. "David, stay with him," I said, though I said it like a question. I carried the worm in a sterile cup out to the resident on call. During the next few hours there was purposeful activity and orders phoned in from specialists, and someone took a Polaroid of the worm next to a ruler for the chart. The man, whose name I cannot remember, went to the intensive care unit, where he died nine days later. Before he died, another seven worms exited his body. They had nested in his pancreas and traveled to his lung, and escaped with his coughs and through the hole his chest tube made. It turned out that over a year earlier the patient had eaten some kind of infested wheat product in the Philippines. All the months between then and when he died, the worms grew and took over his pancreas. He'd lost weight because the parasites wanted everything. When they grew too large for his pancreas they gnawed their way into his chest and that was when his lung collapsed.

I escaped into the body, and the body's mysteries never failed me. There was an element of my father's detective life in the everyday. There was the mystery and the questions, the investigation, and all too often, there was a corpse.

I snorkeled in those days and as I skimmed the surface, eels would surprise me as they slid out of holes in the coral reef with an incoming wave so we would be inches away from each other. Then they would slip back into the darkness. I would think about the man's face when he first saw the worm, how the wriggling worm seemed so much worse than a tumor somehow; we could imagine him dying from a tumor in his pancreas, it was clinical and ordinary for us, but the worms exerted a power that unnerved us all. We wanted a shaman in the room, we wanted candles and sweet oils. I swam with the eels and wanted them to promise that they would stay recessed in their caves while the stunning glass-colored fish swam in schools over my back. My faith was restored in the ocean. God was a sea turtle. He rose with his hard body from the bottom of the green to press against my belly. I wanted to pray, but words fell like stones to the bottom. Far from Esalen and the cabin in the woods, I found my scream and practiced it underwater.

After a year and a few months in Hawaii I had a hard tanned body and a sense of how I might stay in my nursing life and be a poet as well. I had friends in Kaneohe, but I started craving cold air and red leaves and the stunning seasons. A friend told me about traveling nurses. I called an agency in Florida and asked about it. "You tell us where you want to live and we'll see if there is work there," they told me.

Looking at the map was a shopping spree. It was October so it was cold in the north. But I wanted the West, I knew that. "Somewhere in the West," I said. The recruiter told me about a job in Farmington, New Mexico. I looked it up. I liked the location. I had to do paperwork and be interviewed over the phone. The agency FedExed an application packet, which arrived overnight. Two days later, I was offered one of nine positions in San Juan Regional Medical Center. "You won't need a car," the recruiter told me. It was all very organized: I landed in Albuquerque, went to the Capitol Building to get my temporary nursing license, then flew in a puddle jumper to Farmington, where someone from the hospital met me. I was housed, along with the other traveling nurses, in an abandoned wing of the old hospital.

Before I left for New Mexico, I went to New Jersey to see my parents. My father was drinking a lot more now. My mother was tight-lipped and ashamed of him. She didn't cook his meals or do his laundry. She was at her wit's end, and once again I was leaving them. My father was broken and no one knew how to fix him. My sister was my mother's confidant. She carried the burden of everyone's limitations and went to work and had a faithful boyfriend, but you couldn't touch her without startling her.

She had the same boyfriend for many years; his name was Michael. He loved to sing and the two of them belonged to a choral group called Amici Musicorum. They performed concerts with high-spirited hymns in church basements. I envied them their harmonies.

The New Mexico job commitment was only for three months, so even if I hated it, it didn't really matter. I liked this setup. I started to enjoy my frequent going-away parties and coming-home parties and being gone for all the nights when my father was missing or stumbling in stinking of sweet whiskey and cigarettes. I tried to be his ally, to find some way to excuse him, but it got harder every time I was home. One night when I was visiting he tried to enter the apartment quietly but failed and my mother tried to talk to him without waking me. I could hear vague whisperings but nothing really specific until my mother said, "I know! He was my son, too!" Outside my window, a pigeon laid an egg behind a rusty beach chair. The factories under the Pulaski Skyway were toxic and white with fume. Poor bird in the egg. Poor mother bird.

My father stayed sober on the day I left so he could drive me to Newark Airport. I tried to talk to him about what he was doing, but he was flushed and tired looking and didn't want to hear anything I had to say. What did I know about it anyway? I'd gone to Virginia. I wasn't there when my brother got sicker and sicker. I couldn't argue. Almost six years later, my first mistake seemed to be growing in size, not getting smaller, and it occurred to me that New Mexico might not be far enough away.

It became clear pretty early on in Farmington that the reason the recruiter had insisted I didn't need a car was that there was nowhere to go. On the drive from the small regional airport I passed about six taverns, one souvenir shop, a supermarket, and a tire store. It seemed there was one road into town and one road out. Around the hospital there were small houses on streets named after Latin American countries. The nursing supervisor who picked me up at the airport was a polite woman with hard white hair and a beauty mark over her lip like Marilyn Monroe. She pointed out a shop with arrowheads and snake skins. She took me to the closed wing of the hospital and showed me my room, which faced Shiprock National Monument.

As I unpacked in my hospital room I kept my door open. I saw another girl slip out of her room, sneak into one of the empty rooms, and take an extra bedside table. She was looking back and forth like a bad spy in a cheap movie. I waited a few minutes, then knocked on her door. When she opened it I said, "I have no car but I have money for gas." She answered right away, "Great, I have a truck but no gas. Let's go for a ride."

I didn't know it then but I was making one of the best friends of my life. Anne was from Saint Paul, Minnesota, and had been working in Jackson Hole, Wyoming, when she took this position in Farmington. That day we bought wine and drove into the hills around town. We sat on red rock and tried to tell each other the story of our lives. I told her about Johnny on the first day but didn't tell her about my father's drinking. I told her about Hawaii. She told me stories about Saint Paul and her family and a funny story about charcoal briquettes until we were howling in the canyon as loud as coyotes. Anne was tall and strong-boned with wild brown hair in little curls and freckles and a big-toothed smile. I was in awe of her confidence and happiness. We stopped at a 7-Eleven so she could get cigarettes and I watched her from the truck. I couldn't see what she was doing but I saw her go in, then say something to the person at the counter, then turn and say something to another customer by the refrigerator, then soon, all the customers were saying something and laughing. They were *all* laughing. She entered a place where no one was even acknowledging one another and in minutes they were having the time of their

lives. When she got back in the truck I said, "What was that about?"
"What?" she said. "I was just getting cigarettes."

The desert was almost large enough. It was almost hot enough. Sage-
brush lined the road. I danced at the Office Bar night after night, and
swam naked in Navajo Lake in private inlets among red stone. The
lake was a meadow, was an ice-cold cup of forgiveness. The grief that
I had been holding in my legs and in my back fell away with each
stroke, with each underwater dive. Overhead, birds made circles in
their mating and tipped back on tree branches. Out on the lake, a
speedboat zoomed past carrying all the mistakes I'd made so far. On
the cliffs I found a leather scraper and a tool for beading. I found a
turtle shell that I carried in my pack. I was slowly turning from the
bodies in the beds and looking carefully at the rest of the world.

Every morning I looked out at Shiprock and imagined the large
rock bird carrying Indians to this safe place. The bird's head at the
top of the rock turned this way and that in the sun. Most amazingly, I
worked on a general med-surg floor, which meant that people came in
with broken legs, spider bites, rattlesnake bites, lung infections. They
had their stories that they told with humor. And then, remarkably,
they got better and went home and I would see them again at the car
wash or the green market. Sometimes they had ski poles on the car
when I saw them, or fishing gear. Where were all the dying boys?

Anne and I worked Monday through Friday, the 3:00 p.m. to 11:00
p.m. shift. During the week we ate crackers and drank the little juices
on the patient carts and saved all our money for Friday night, when
we raced the fifty-one miles to Durango, Colorado, for last call at the
Pelican Bar. We camped out or stayed in a hotel, and on Saturday we
rented jeeps and drove all the various trails between Durango and
Telluride. We went dancing at night and sometimes I met a boy I

liked enough to sleep with—a rodeo guy, a baseball player. Then we'd head back on Sunday night and start the workweek all over again. In a way I still escaped into the body. The boys I made love to reminded me of all that my brother lost, of all the experiences he didn't get to have. I was puzzled by my happiness and wondered if I was being unfaithful to him.

Clara was a nurse's aide who was Navajo. She gave me a doll and a handmade silver name badge with a jasper stone embedded over my name. She taught me simple phrases to use with the older patients who spoke only Navajo. We made rounds together and turned people from one side to the other, straightened their sheets, and massaged their backs. Clara was quiet and had small rituals: a way to line up pitchers for ice, a certain method of folding back the blanket on the bed. We worked well together and I listened to her instincts about patients. "This one is carrying a weakness in her legs," she might say to me. Or, "The woman in bed four is on fire, but her feet are cold." Something or someone had given her wisdom about the body. I trusted her. So night after night, we walked the halls together.

Every weekend Anne and I drove into the mountains where trees were bent from snow runoff in spring. Every Sunday night we made our way back to Farmington. To the red rocks and dry sage. It reminded me of the first year I lived on my own in Charlottesville. There was beauty all around me, and the strange excess of space made sense to me. It was, after all, a world without my brother.

One night I dreamt I was falling from a cliff and was going to die. In the dream I reassured myself that I couldn't really die in the dream, because to do that meant, according to legend, that I would die in real life. But then I did die. I didn't wake up and I hit an abyss and everything was very black and I understood the endless falling of a new kind of fear. I was unnerved. I looked out the window in the morning toward Shiprock and, instead of a ship of Indians carried to safety, I saw people dropped into a desert where the earth was dry and nothing would grow and people suffered in the tar pits and uranium mines. The whisper of yellow buds in the meadow seemed to mock their circumstance. The crows were picking at them. The sun scorched their backs.

That evening Clara noticed that I was not myself, and on a break, I finally told her about the dream. "That dream means that you are spiritually barren," she said. "You must do something about it as soon as you can—you are very vulnerable to bad spirits when you are open like this. This dream was a warning to you." I knew enough about Clara by now not to take what she said lightly.

When my brother died, our pastor, Father Divine, came to meet with us at the funeral parlor. "I have something I really want you to say," I told him. "It can be either at church or at the funeral home, but it's really important to me." I gave him the Elizabeth Bishop poem "One Art." I had it in a book flagged with a big cloth bookmark. There was a stanza that I particularly loved. Would it make sense to the others? I didn't care. It was the words I wanted to send on to my brother, floating there, above us all:

> —Even losing you (the joking voice, a gesture
> I love) I shan't have lied. It's evident
> the art of losing's not too hard to master
> though it may look like (*Write* it!) like disaster.

He agreed to read the poem. He was sweating with fake compassion, and leaned in too close, and laid his solicitous hand on my shoulder. My sister's boyfriend, Mike, sang Bob Dylan's "Blowin' in the Wind." My father brought up the bread and wine for the Eucharist, and my mother was a shiny pearl in her sad cocoon. I sat and waited for the poem, which never came. I followed the casket in the pouring rain to the cemetery, and it was cold, and I thought maybe now he would say it. He never read those words to my brother for me, and I was stupefied and angry and too shy to demand it or ask for my book back. Everyone was gushing over him in his haughty priestness, and I thought it was sacrilegious that he was named Divine. I made my way out of the burial area and cursed his round belly and his soft, fake face. Behind me, the ground swallowed my brother whole. The rain was a knife, was a cold knife twisting in my chest. My faith flew from me like bats dropped from a cave. It was a *whoosh* and a *zoom* and a *howl* as it left. I was so young you couldn't tell by looking at me that I was just a shell because I still had good hair and clear skin and danced in circles to Spanish music and the flowers on my dresses were a testimony of some kind that turned out to be a lie. Sometimes when I was stripped naked in Navajo Lake, buried in the cold green water up to my neck, in a hole dug in sacred ground, a darkness would open its arms and hold me in its rocking waves.

The same day Clara told me that my soul was in trouble we had two emergency admissions. One was a young Navajo man who was working in the mines when a vat of tar blew up and burned his chest and arms. The other was a man who was driving drunk and flipped his truck. His legs were broken and he had a compression fracture of his spine, but he wasn't paralyzed. He still smelled of beer and dust, and his three-year-old son was missing. He didn't remember whether or not he had taken the son with him. The wife was out with friends and now no one could find the boy. He wasn't home and he wasn't with the truck.

The intensive care unit was packed but both of these admissions needed a lot of care, so instead of the six or eight patients I normally had, our charge nurse gave me just those two, in private rooms, side by side. Frank was the Indian boy's name and he needed dressing changes every two hours. The dressing changes required strict isola-

tion to prevent infection from setting in, so between gowning and
ungowning, washing and gloving and doing the dressing, it took an
hour every two hours to complete. In between I was watching Ben,
the drunk driver, for signs of concussion and cleaning the external
pin sites holding his legs together. His legs were in traction and the
weights hung freely from the edge of the bed. He had a triangular
pulley he could use to shift himself in bed. He had a lot of cuts and
scrapes that needed cleaning, a urine catheter, a tube in his nose to
keep his stomach empty and two IV lines, one for fluids, one for antibiotics and steroids. He was complaining. I could barely stand to look
at him. His wife, even knowing their son was lost, sat by his side and
prayed and forgave him before they even knew what had happened.
He didn't ask for forgiveness and I saw my father's lowest point when I
looked at him. I didn't like this man and I loved my father, and seeing
them in each other put me in a foul mood.

But then I scrubbed and gowned and gloved and opened white
gauzes onto a sterile field in Frank's room. He wouldn't take a lot of
pain medicine because he had two uncles who were drug addicts. I
tried to reassure him but he was firm. I prepared the Silvadene cream
and the cleaning solvent for the dressing. I watched his face as I undressed the burns. I could see him try to leave the center of pain and
our silence in the room became all about him staying clear in his
mind. I attempted to be as gentle as possible. I felt his body relax
under my hands as the last wrap was in place. In just over an hour we
would begin again.

In Ben's room I washed and cleaned the pin sites, the places where
the hardware entered his bones. He writhed and caused the traction
weights to shift and hit the bed, which yanked the bone placement
and caused a spasm. "You can't move like that," I said. He heard
through his beard and his dirty skin that I didn't care about his
pain. It was true. I thought there was not suffering enough for him.
His wife had three teeth missing in the front and a strawberry-print
blouse that was stretched across her skinny back by the curve of her

malnourished spine. She looked like a drinker too, but maybe a re-formed drinker because her hygiene was good and she seemed alert and there was no smell to her except the smell of coffee. I was not as kind to her as I should have been. Why aren't you looking for your baby? I wanted to ask her. In the medication room I checked in with Anne, who was really busy since the other nurses had to take all my extra patients.

"What a bastard," I said.

"How's the burn guy?" she asked.

"He's a fuckin' saint," I told her.

Midway through the shift a state trooper came down the hall. He caught me about to enter Frank's room for another dressing change. He wanted me to go with him into Ben's room. I told Frank I'd be a few minutes and headed in. The trooper shook his head at me as we entered, as if to say not good, this isn't good, which I knew of course, the minute I saw him.

Ben's little three-year-old son had been in the truck, unbelted, no car seat, and he'd gone flying out of the truck when Ben drove off the road. His nearly weightless body kept flying down into the can-yon and he landed face down in a muddy puddle where he died. The trooper told Ben and his wife, who was tugging on the front of her strawberry blouse and rolling her tongue in the space where her teeth were missing. Ben grabbed her for comfort and she turned to ease his distress, and I was so angry I could barely stand still. "I gotta go," I said to the trooper. He nodded and I rolled my eyes at him as I left. He knew. He spent most of his time with assholes like this. And then I realized both sides of my father were in the one room. The good trooper and the stupid drunk. And now both of them had a dead son. I was almost craving going to Frank's room, where we would silently clean and cover his raw skin. Our breathing and concentration were a meditation on suffering, like the stations of the cross. This was the third dressing of the shift and it was hard to believe, but I could al-ready see a slight filling in around the edges of the burns. The web of his dignity and healing made a cocoon around me while I was with him. Outside, the summer sun was setting behind red rock and the occasional cloud drifted in a pink fluff at the edge of the bluffs.

The only way I could keep Frank all week was to keep Ben all week, and so I did. Dozens of people came and went to console Ben. Someone actually took Polaroids at the funeral so he could see pictures of his son in the coffin. I tried my best not to look him in the eye. He would raise himself up with the pulley when I slid a clean sheet under him. I never tried to find out what it was about him that kept so many loyal friends and family in his corner. I should have; but all I could see was his careless turn of the wheel and the little blond child go flying.

Frank had only two visitors, his mother and father. They were both so short they only came up to his armpits when they stood alongside him, and they had to wear gowns and masks when they were in the room. His father walked with a cane and his mother wore the many-layered skirts of the old Navajo. She had a turquoise belt with a stone the size of a lemon. By the end of the week we were able to take Frank off isolation. Without the masks I could see his parents' faces, and they were the faces of so many hard stories. I had the desire to kneel next to them. I taught the mother how to change his dressing and she was as quiet and as careful as I had been. Her willingness to do the dressings meant Frank could go home. Frank and I had barely said anything to each other all week and yet, when he was dressing and I was helping him work a loose T-shirt over his head, he paused and hugged me. I knew I couldn't cry, but I found it too hard to speak so I just rested my hand on his arm a little longer than necessary and I think he knew how much I had loved the time in his room, in warm coveralls and latex gloves, quietly watching his skin repair itself. On Friday I told the charge nurse, "Someone else has to take care of that asshole from the wreck." I was focused on the late-night drive to

Durango and the dancing and drinking and maybe, if I was lucky, I would run into Rob, the rodeo guy I liked the most, and when we were having sex I could imagine Frank's body with its pink patches hovering over me.

The thing I realized about the dream and about Frank is that what Clara said was true. I felt like an old metal cup at a campsite, empty and smashed. I was living outside the fire that was faith, and I realized for the first time that I had to work to get back inside the flame. Going to church wouldn't do it. I knew from the quick betrayal of Father Divine that I didn't want to trust someone like that again. No, I needed to find faith outside the structure of a congregation. I didn't know how to begin, but I thought the banks of the San Juan River would be as good a place as any. The weekend after Frank left the hospital, Anne and I went camping and agreed to meet a couple of friends from work there, but just as we got to the river and pitched our tents the rain came down and red ants ran from the hill between our tents. Craig, a friend from the hospital, had cooked trout and brought us some. In my state of mind it was the fish of the apostles and it tasted like a holy meat dipped in salt. The longer the day got, the wetter it got, and finally Anne and I decided a Best Western with a Jacuzzi might be closer to God. We left just as there was a break in the cloud cover.

Halfway to the highway the truck's accelerator stuck at about five miles an hour. We were afraid that if we stopped we wouldn't make it home, so we drove on the shoulder. Eventually some guy drove up alongside us and convinced us to stop. "You'll get killed," he said, and got under the truck and worked mud from the accelerator. He fixed the problem in just a few minutes and we offered to buy him a drink back in town. We arranged to meet at Drummond's Bar. He brought a friend who was light blond, tan, and six foot nine. I wore a pale yellow skirt with a white blouse and a little pin of Saint Teresa on the collar. Anne was in jeans and a plaid flannel shirt and they all played pool while I watched Mark, the tall one, move around the table. After last call I drove up to the bluffs overlooking town with Mark. I sat next to him on the rocks. His hand completely enclosed mine. The sky opened like a black blanket with little holes poking through. I declared my faith in his kiss and I practiced my religion for a long time in the black night with the click of insects in the air and this tall man holding me against him and below us the town went to sleep except for the occasional light in a window.

The next evening the nursing supervisor called me to tell me some guy had been trying to locate me, but *he didn't know your last name,* she said with a tone of disapproval. I asked her for the number and even though I only had nine weeks left in New Mexico, I thought I would release all the grief I had been holding on to with this man. Maybe I wouldn't have to enter church in my search for something big to believe in. Clara didn't think this would stop the dreams of falling into blackness.

What I didn't find was love everlasting. What I did find was a body separate from my family, separate from my brother. I found a way to make love with my legs to the sky: nothing, not even the dome of tent, could contain them. I found Mark's body and all the mysteries of his skin. He had a knife scar across his back and a mark over his left nipple from where someone scorched him with a branding iron. After a few weeks, I realized he dealt homegrown pot from Colorado, which explained his money, his nice apartment, and his ability to sleep in. He wore his bed quilt like a cape when he danced naked down the stairs, and when we made love we laughed and laughed. I entered one part of my faith, not the whole thing, but I entered a boy who wasn't dying, though death had sought him out; he was golden, and a leaping deer, and I took back joy, the first step to closing the hole that my soul was edging toward. My dreams turned into dreams of flying, were dreams of skin and water, and the only darkness I saw was the regret in my own soul when I closed my eyes against the body of a dangerous man.

There came a time when I thought I might be pregnant. Anne asked me what birth control I used. "Well, I'm really regular," I said. I saw her skepticism. We went to the lake and I cataloged my symptoms: sore breasts, late period, nausea. I refused to talk about it any further. There were no over-the-counter tests then and it was a Sunday and I was only three weeks late. Navajo Lake had no beach and had one boat slip, but if you took some of the dirt roads around the lake you could climb down the rocks into little private swimming coves. We found our favorite one and took off our clothes. The rocks were sun warmed and smooth. We lay back for a bit. I was thinking about my parents and how horrible it would be to be pregnant. I knew if I showed up with a baby they would accept it, but I didn't want that life and I didn't want a drug dealer for my baby's father and I really didn't ever want to give birth. I had never been one of those women who craved that experience. So I decided I would pray, and I did. And in the act of praying I found that I never really lost the girl who made altars. Then I stood up and jumped into the cold flat lake. Anne jumped in right after me and we were laughing and waving across the lake to some naked people we could barely see but who we thought were waving back. We spent the day playing with a log we found in the water and talking about what kind of assignment we would take next. Anne was thinking of Miami, but I was unsure. I didn't want to go to Florida, but I didn't want to think about being away from Anne. I agreed to call the agency soon.

When we got back that day I realized I had gotten my period. It was a little heavier than usual, but I had no cramps. The nausea and the sore breasts went away and I didn't know for sure, but I thought that it might have been God naked and waving on the rocks across the water.

Private Duty

I WAS BACK EAST WAITING FOR ANNE TO FINISH HER MIAMI job. She was trying to get the Farmington hospital to give us two more assignments. Flying nurse assignments were in twelve-week blocks. After each twelve weeks the company usually gave us the option of signing up for another twelve weeks. Sometimes re-signing came with a bonus. In Farmington, they unexpectedly stopped using flying nurses toward the end of our last assignment. Anne was determined to talk them into hiring us again. Meanwhile, I moved back to New Jersey, worked with a temp agency, and lived with my parents in their apartment. I did private-duty shifts for twelve hours at night. I didn't like private duty; I felt uncomfortable sitting at people's bedsides, and I felt that I wasn't working hard enough for the money I was making.

While I was away my father had entered rehab and had been in AA for thirty days. He embraced AA meetings at first, then made mosaic projects, then collected baseball cards, until one day he let his obsessions go and just eased into the body of a father who walked to the grocery store holding my mother's hand. He stayed sober for the rest of his life until the week he was dying, when he decided we all needed Italian food and good red wine around his bed. But at this point, he was at the peak of his AA work, going to meetings every night and drinking coffee in diners afterward with people none of us knew. My mother was still anxious because he went out every night after supper and we weren't convinced when he got home he would be sober. She spent long hours alone and sometimes I felt like I was getting closer to her, but then out of the blue she would say, "You don't know, you were in Virginia!" Or now, substitute Virginia for New

Mexico for Hawaii. It seemed as though I was missing all the life back home by trying to have one of my own, and the recriminations were piling up. It became too hard for her to explain the things I'd missed. So my father gathered in a room to talk to strangers about his loneliness, and my mother crocheted colorful threads in her lap, and I sat in the rocking chair, with all my secrets and all my regrets.

During this time, I got a private-duty assignment in a brownstone in Greenwich Village. Enid was forty-two years old and dying of ovarian cancer. She wanted to die at home, and her husband, who was almost sixty, wanted her to get her wish. They moved a bed to a downstairs room. They had two little dogs and her husband walked around the house with a white cockatiel on his shoulder. He was kind. He delicately carried his wooden pipe around the house, the scent of him wafting before and after his movement through the rooms. He was holding their life story in his hands. He held it over her in the bed and she tried to look up at him, but the pain pulled from the center of her and curled her into a ball and fluids poured out from between her legs. I spent most of my time keeping Enid clean and dry and giving her shots of morphine or little liquid doses in children's cups. Her husband wanted them to watch their life like a movie, to help her remember their happiness. But their happiness was locked in the backyard by pain, which was taking over the room. Enid's body lost whatever fat it had and she slid her hand out from under the gown and wrapped it around my wrist as though she was taking my pulse. I felt my veins pulse against her bones and I wanted to find a way to raise her up into the love her husband had for her. His devotion to her was as tangible as the white bird on his shoulder when he paced the room.

A friend of Enid's from Germany came to visit. She was a pharmacist and she studied the various tubes and creams and fixated on everything we threw in the garbage. She started interrogating me about how the chemicals would break down and where the garbage went, and behind her Enid was writhing in the bed and folding up into a ball. Her husband and I joined forces and demanded more pain relief from her doctor. Over eleven days when I came and went and held her hips up over the bed, we got control of the pain. "She will sleep more," I told him. He accepted this, anything to not see the snake of the pain twisting in her pelvis. Her face was stunning even in its illness. She was a fawn trying to stand. She was a curtain, she blew in and out of the room.

On the eleventh night I entered the house and the day nurse told me she thought Enid might die. I moved closer to Enid, and noticed that her legs, which were almost always pulled up close to her, were relaxed out in front of her and fell away from the center of her body, her feet facing out. She was dazed but awake and she smiled at me. Her husband entered the room, the animals at his side. He was crying and sat next to us. Outside we had our first snow of the season, big flakes under the streetlight that made shadows in the room like bubbles on the wall. The white feathery bird on his shoulder watched the change in light and at one point leaned its head toward the husband's head in commiseration. The dogs whimpered and slid under the bed. The room was a ship about to leave the dock. We had done well. Enid was home, her pain ebbed, and over the next four hours, her breathing changed. The rhythm of her body uncoiled and her skin took on fever, a kind of metabolic excitement.

I left him alone with her and sat in the kitchen. I found myself looking at the bottles of pills and tubes of ointments and creams. Maybe the German woman was right to worry. So much goes into the earth. Behind the pills snow piled against the glass. I heard a sound like a boat grinding against the water's wake. It was Enid's husband sobbing. She left him in the snow. The white bird carried her from the room. I timed my return to him based on the clock of something I understand but can't explain. I eased him from her, and called the day nurse, who would have had trouble traveling in the snow. We called her family. I made him tea, which he traded for a scotch on the rocks. I called the funeral home for him, and I washed Enid one last time and put a clean sheet beneath her. The vision of her collar bone in the light of the new snow, the way it collected her last drops of sweat, is what I took with me. I didn't see her husband ever again, but he should know I never forgot her, or the sacred invitation they extended to me over those eleven nights.

When I left their home it was light out. The snow had stopped falling and was packed and bright on the city streets. I decided to walk to the train. My white shoes in the snow made a new path on the street. I remembered why I loved being a nurse. I loved the gift of being with someone as she transcended suffering. Of helping her in small ways: turning her in the bed, or placing a blanket over her legs. It is during these tiny moments of attention that you can see the release of the person's hold on the body. A sort of resignation enters the eyes and breath eases out for one final time. The room to me then is as blessed as any church.

At the entrance to the Ninth Street PATH station a man was playing guitar and on the corner, Balducci's opened its stalls of fresh fruit. The bread in the window was golden. I went down into the tunnel and made my way home to my parents' house. I slept, and when I woke, I called Anne in Miami and tried to figure out where to go next.

Anne managed the impossible. She talked the hospital into creating two contracts with our travel company, one for each of us. We returned to Farmington three weeks later. My parents thought I was out of my mind. I started making the rounds of good-bye drinks and little parties. The friends I was leaving had started getting married, buying houses, and some even had babies. I could still fit everything I owned in a big green nylon duffle. I packed my typewriter; I had started writing again. Once again, my father drove me to the airport. My mother stayed home, her disappointment in me as large as a cathedral. It soared and was cavernous and fearsome and filled with the chorus of all I'd done wrong.

Anne and I were scheduled to work on separate units this time. Anne was in the ICU and I was back on med-surg, but we had the same great schedule of evenings with every weekend off. I bought an old U.S. Geological Survey truck at auction. It was a light-blue Dodge Ram with the shadow of *Geological Survey* still on the side door, which added to its charm. Anita, our charge nurse, decided she wanted us to meet her son, who had just moved to Farmington. Anne and I were dreading it, but we went for Anita, because she was good to us. Randy turned out to be a tall, handsome man. Anne and I looked at each other and we both began flirting with him. It became clear early on that they were perfect for each other.

We still took our weekend trips, but Mark, my blond drug dealer, had moved to Phoenix. When Anne was out with Randy during the week, I spent more time alone in my hospital room, raising and lowering the head of the bed with the automatic handheld control and thinking about where I would go after New Mexico. I asked the red clay eagle flying out of Shiprock Monument and realized I hadn't answered the question about faith yet. Every night carried the danger of the black slit, the little hole that my soul might fall through.

One night about a month after we got back to Farmington, there was a big accident involving three cars and a motorcycle. The first few patients went to ICU and then there were no more beds in the unit. We got two patients on the med-surg floor. The boy on the motorcycle hadn't been wearing a helmet. He was brain dead but was being kept alive on a respirator until his family could come from Colorado and we could ask them about donating his organs. He had slid on his back when he crashed and so his face was untouched and stunningly handsome, but the back of his head was gone and was packed with a kind of gel bandage. When we transferred him from the ambulance stretcher to the bed, the respiratory therapist and I were both at his head, one securing the breathing tube to attach to the bedside machine and one to steady the pillow behind his head. Clara, the nursing assistant, stayed in the room with him. She was told to call us if anything beeped on any of the machines, while the police in Colorado made their way in the rain to his parents' house.

The other patient was a girl who had been on the back of the motorcycle. She looked remarkably like me. At least *to me* she did; no one else seemed to notice the resemblance. First, she slid against and then under the Buick, and the jagged bumper and the force of her slide caused a disarticulation, a traumatic amputation of her leg at the hip. The orthopedic doctor on call took me into the room. The girl was in and out of consciousness. The ambulance driver said at the scene she kept asking about her leg, at one point saying, "I can't feel it, it's broken, isn't it?" The doctor showed me what he wanted me to do as they got the OR ready. He took my gloved hands and covered them in mitts of Kerlix gauze and shoved my fist into her bone socket. "She needs to stop losing blood," he told me. "We'll get the room ready as fast as we can," he said. "Stay like this until I send for her." He left me bent over the edge of her bed and as the minutes passed my hand started to get numb and a pulling pain started in my shoulder.

It was a traumatic marriage, my hand to the cave of her bone, and from time to time she moaned, or started to open her eyes. Then we would watch each other, but she was too weak to raise herself fully awake or to question my close attention. Underneath my latexed fist, her blood slowly seeped from her hip bone. I waited for almost twenty-five minutes, and when the OR was ready I walked alongside her while three other people rolled the bed. We passed the room with the dead boy. Clara was sitting beside him touching his hand, as though he was still there, and he was of course, and I respected her for that. By the end of the night we had released them both to the OR, his parents having said yes to his heart, his kidneys, his skin.

Anne and Randy and I went out drinking after work. Anne was glowing. I saw someone I thought was cute playing darts, but I also felt the stain of the girl on my arm and decided I wouldn't abandon her so easily. I went back to my room at the hospital and Anne and Randy went to the playground, where they played on the swings and began their arc of flying toward each other forever.

My dignity began to unravel during the second assignment in Farmington. I went out with a man in a black cowboy hat named Jimmy. I went out with an FBI agent who had a broken leg and was on medical leave. I went out with a guy who lived in a trailer and hunted with a bow and arrow. One night when Anne and I were in a diner after last call at the Office Bar, the manager of the diner announced over the intercom, "Will the girl in the flowered dress please meet the man in the parking lot?" I look around. I was the only one with flowers. Anne was shaking her head. The waitress came over. "It's you, honey," she said. "Go see what the boy wants."

I went to the parking lot with my gray and red flowered dress, with the shiny silver edging around the neck. There was a good-looking guy standing next to his truck.

"Would you come to Colorado Springs with me?" he asked.

"Well, no," I told him. "I don't even know you."

"Would you smoke a joint with me, get to know me, and come to Colorado Springs?"

"You know, really, no thanks," I said. "I have to go."

He called after me, "I knew you in another life!"

I went back into the diner and saw Jimmy at one table and the FBI agent at another. They both looked up. I nodded to them and sat back down. "What a psycho that was," I said to Anne. I think he must have sensed the sexual energy I was throwing out all over, the body hunger I seemed to have for everyone all of a sudden. The general hunger, I should say. I did everything to extremes: eating, dancing, drinking, and stacking up men until, like now, in a small town, two of them were in the diner at the same time.

"I've got to leave this town soon," I said to Anne.

A week or so after the incident in the diner I went to a party with the FBI guy. I can't remember his name, but I remember the cast on his leg, which opened a little cut on my shin when we were making love. There were always men who wanted to date the traveling nurses. Formula for love: be leaving town in three months. The party was in the hills outside town in a stucco house. I was tired because I had worked late the night before, and instead of going to sleep, Anne and I had spent the day at Navajo Lake and I'd gotten too much sun. Midway through the party I wanted to leave, but he wanted to stay. "You can lie down in the bedroom and I'll come get you," he said. It seemed like a good idea and so I went to the back of the house where a queen-size water bed was covered with a leopard print comforter. I sank down in the center and fell sound asleep.

I woke to two men I didn't know, one on either side of me, touching me. Suddenly, I was Spider-Man. My instincts were as sharp as a leather scraper. My elbows angled out, one to each side, and I flew into the air in the center of them and out of the bed. "What do you think you're going to do . . . rape me!?" I yelled. My fists were balls in the air and my legs were squared with my shoulders. The men stared at me as I backed out of the room.

I loved my body for its unexpected flight. I loved the adrenaline that turned my face red and sent my heart galloping in my chest. I went to the kitchen, where I found my date eating scrambled eggs. "Really great fucking FBI agent," I said. "Let's go." He dropped me at the hospital and I never spoke to him again. In my own bed I tried to revive my action-hero moves to show Anne, but it was physically impossible. Outside the window, stars fell like silver minnows in a stream.

Anne and I started talking about the next assignment, since ours would run out in December and that was only two months away. I could tell she was in love with Randy, but the hospital wasn't going to use travelers at all anymore, and if we wanted to stay we had to accept full-time jobs. Neither one of us wanted to settle in Farmington. I heard about an assignment in Savannah, Georgia, and she and I both interviewed for positions there.

One day we took all our laundry to a place on the reservation. My truck needed a new battery, so I stopped at the car parts store and picked one up. I figured I could change it while our laundry was being done. We each had three washers: I had all my scrubs in one, underwear and towels in another, and fourteen Laura Ashley dresses on a cold, delicate cycle in the third. We went outside to deal with the truck. When we came back in I headed to the machines, which were empty. At first, I thought I had the wrong row, but Anne's machines were also empty. We went from one machine to the other in the four rows of washers. Not a single piece of clothing was left. We started asking the people there, "What happened? What did you see?" We got shrugs and simple Navajo phrases back. Even the young people were pretending they didn't speak English. I was crazed and called the tribal police from a pay phone. After about forty minutes a deputy came to take a report. Anne and I had to go to work in less than an hour and the only clothes we had were the ones on our backs. The deputy took our names and the estimated value of what had been in each machine. I tried to explain about Laura Ashley dresses. He didn't get it. I told him I planned to stake out the Laundromat and said, "If I see a Navajo woman wearing a Laura Ashley print I am going to knock her down and rip it off her back."

He looked at me and closed his notebook. "Ma'am, making this report does not give you the right to do violence to the Native American population." I was dumbfounded. Grieving. Three of the dresses were white, two in discontinued patterns. Anne and I went to the hospital where they agreed to lend us OR scrubs. Our travel company sent us each a check for two hundred and fifty dollars so we could buy some new clothes. But suddenly I was tired of Farmington, already thinking about Georgia, about being near the beach.

My father came to meet me at Newark Airport. I loved time alone with him. He looked good, and I knew right away he hadn't been drinking. His neck had its shape back and he was trim in a Columbo trench coat. I was starting to miss him more every time I left. He was excited for me about the Savannah job and like everything else, he knew things about the town and the history of the area and the river there. He loved to travel and see new things, but my mother was content to go to Maine every summer vacation and, except for a rare trip here and there, that's what they did. Maine was a landscape she understood. The rocks were jagged and unforgiving, the spray of waves dramatic. The ocean from the cliff was too rough for swimmers; she could stand at the ocean and not see a young boy laughing in the waves. She could look out and see an empty world of water, just like the world she lived in.

My father took my bag at the airport and we started scheming a way for my parents to visit Georgia in the spring. The outline of downtown Jersey City and the World Trade Center across the water rose from the turnpike exit. We stopped to pick up grave blankets for the cemetery and then headed down to Holy Name Cemetery to lay them on the ground. My father had the tools for this chore. He always had a ball of twine, a curl of wire, bolt cutters, boxes of nails. He was meticulously ready. He put the pine blankets on my aunt Anne's grave, the Kelly family grave, and finally, on my brother's headstone, where he also tied a wreath with a simple red bow. He took his cap off. There was ice in the air and the smell of sewer from the Duncan Projects, which lay just beyond the west fence. Trucks rocketed past on Highway 440. I understood then my need to live somewhere beautiful; the wire and dust and ice of this city were like a thorn in my thumb. It pricked and it stung.

When my father parked behind their apartment building and turned off the car I decided to ask him something I had always wanted to know. "Dad, did you ever have nightmares?" I told him about the girl and her leg and the beautiful boy with the missing skull. He didn't move to leave the car and then he told me a story about something that haunted him.

"When I was a new cop, only on the force a couple of weeks, there was this guy, an old Jewish guy that worked at Colgate-Palmolive and he decided to give this black guy a ride home, and remember, Mare, at that time he would've been a Negro and it was kind of a political statement the old man was makin'. Anyway, they hit the intersection of Fourth and Erie just as a truck went through the stop sign headed for the Holland Tunnel. The thing is, Mare, I should've shielded the old guy because he didn't look too badly hurt. But I didn't think of it, so when I asked him how he was, he said, 'Well, I'm OK, but I don't know about my buddy here,' and then he turned. Well, the black guy had gone through the windshield, remember there were no seat belts in those days, and his head had been cut off. It had landed on the hood of the car and actually . . ."—my father hesitated—"spun around so it was facing the car. The old guy turned, saw the shredded body, then saw the head on the hood looking right at him, and well, Mare, he died right there, from the shock of it. I should've protected him, you know, but I didn't."

The car was a velvety confessional. My father had finally talked to me like I was one of the cops in the precinct house. His story made a cocoon for us in the old Ford. "I still have nightmares about that one," he said. We nodded at each other and got my bag and went up to see my mother. I never had the nightmare about either the girl or the boy again, and I wonder sometimes if my father took them on as well, as he took on so many other things in the world.

My mother opened the door and was pink and pretty and shorter than she was when I saw her last. I was surprised to realize that I was happy to be home. She looked at my skirt and said, "Honey, take that off, I'll hem it a little, you have nice legs, you should show them more."

My father passed behind her and winked at me. It was an old habit, her attempts to tailor my loose gauzy wardrobe.

"All my Laura Ashley dresses were stolen," I said, in an attempt to change the subject.

My father decided to stir things up a bit. "Check out the muck-a-luck boots she has on under that skirt, Margie."

I was home and all the old feelings were stirred up. Behind my mother a black-and-white picture of my brother leaning on a wall. My sister would come for dinner, but we wouldn't be all together again ever.

I Love a Soldier

I love thee to the level of every day's
Most quiet need, by sun and candle-light.
I love thee freely, as men strive for Right;
I love thee purely, as they turn from Praise.
I love thee with the passion put to use
In my old griefs, and with my childhood's faith.

—ELIZABETH BARRETT BROWNING

THE MINUTE THE LAURA ASHLEY DRESSES WERE STOLEN I didn't know how to present myself to the world. Laura Ashley dresses in those days looked like pioneer clothing, tight bodices with wide skirts, all in the delicate flowered patterns of antique quilts. It was about hiding the body. It was about pretending the times we lived in were simpler. I thought the dresses were romantic, but I realize now, they were a woman's idea of romance. Men wanted to see angles and tight pants, or short dresses with high heels. I was suddenly faced with the opportunity to re-create the physical self I would show the world and so I bought a mishmash of things: some loose dresses that I wore with Frye boots and leg warmers, but I also wore navy blue sweatpants and tight T-shirts. I realized I liked the feel of pants cinched at my waist, or tucking my head into a hooded sweatshirt. I wanted, I realized, to look like everyone else. In New Mexico, I attracted men precisely because I wore dresses in a town where the women wore blue jeans and flannel shirts. Now I was heading to Savannah, where women dressed up for the supermarket, and I was stocking up on gym clothes. I wondered if I would ever find a place where I would feel at home just the way I was.

Anne met me at the airport. She'd driven into town earlier the same day. The traveling company had leased a row of cute apartments with a pool on the edge of the city where thirty or so nurses would live side by side. The other apartments in the complex were filled with Army Rangers since Savannah was home to Hunter Army Airfield. The Rangers had great haircuts: short on top but shaved around the sides and back. The town was filled with men who were fit and serious. I decided I would do everything to avoid another romance. I wanted time to be by myself.

Anne and I went to a bar by the river and I told her, "I am not going to date anyone in this town." I noticed a group of French sailors dancing together. One American Ranger had joined them. I loved to dance; I headed onto the dance floor and just joined them. They were a happy group. I was glad no one was trying to talk, just smiling and dancing to the live band. After a while the American guy made his way to me. He tried to say something about the music.

"I don't want to talk," I said.

"Can I buy you a drink?" he shouted in my ear.

"As long as you don't talk to me," I told him.

Anne was content at the bar, talking to two other traveling nurses who had come in. She raised her eyebrows when she saw me sitting with this guy who was handing me a white wine, but I just shook my head reassuringly. He was trying to tell me things about himself. "I don't want to know anything," I had to say a few times before he stopped. He just watched me drink my wine and smiled a few times. Then I was ready to dance again. When Anne was ready to leave she signaled to me.

"Can I walk you to your car?" he asked.

"I have a truck."

"Can I walk you to your truck?"

"I don't need you to," I said. I kept walking and he kept alongside Anne and me. Occasionally he took a little skip like a happy child.

"Can I call you?"

"Look," I told him, "I just got to town. I don't have a phone." We were standing outside my truck. "Just don't worry about it."

"Where do you live?" he said.

"Pine Hollow," I told him. I closed the truck door and gave him a little wave. All I'd told him was the name of the complex of something like two hundred apartments. Anne was driving and she shifted into gear. "Happy birthday," she said.

Savannah was a lush place with high humidity and exorbitant flowers. January could be cold, but that year it wasn't. The temperature the next day was almost sixty degrees. Anne and I had made a conscious decision not to live together because we were such good friends. At the time it seemed brilliant, but now that we each had three roommates we didn't know, and we were spending all our time going back and forth between each other's apartments, it seemed crazy. One of her roommates wanted to check out Tybee Island, about thirty minutes east of town, so we decided to go in her car. Savannah smelled like wet paper from the mill, but as we headed out of the city it started to smell sweeter, and the air felt good on our dry desert skin. We would be starting work in four days. I was going to be on night shift on the eye, ear, nose, and throat floor and Anne was scheduled for nights on the neurology floor. We were both at a private hospital in a nice part of town. We hated nights, but those were the only shifts available.

Later that day, when we got back from the beach, my roommate Doris said, "Some guy Mike's been by here." I was puzzled.

"Anne? Did we meet a Mike last night?"

She wasn't sure. "What was the name of that guy you were dancing with?"

"God, I don't know," I said. "I didn't let him talk to me."

"Well," Doris said, "he's coming back at five."

The boy at the door was the boy from the dance floor. He wanted to go to Ruby Tuesday for a drink. I shrugged OK, then asked him how he found out where I lived. "Well," he said, "I saw your big blue truck

parked outside and then just knocked on a few doors." I didn't know
whether to be flattered or scared. "Listen," I said, "let's take separate
cars. I don't know enough about you to drive with you." And off we
went.

The mystery was about the body and the body's touch. I understood
how the body died, but until Mike and I were sitting side by side an
hour later and talking, and his knee touched my knee, I realized I
knew nothing about how the body lived. I had made love to boys I
liked, to boys I thought I loved, and to men I barely knew. I liked the
energy of sex, and the way it allowed me to lose the faces of the boys
who died, and even, sometimes, to lose my brother's face. But nothing
prepared me for what happened with Mike. He felt it too, I could tell
by the way his face changed into a bird, into a lake. I saw myself in
the flying water all around him. We left his VW Rabbit at the bar and
took my truck to the woods at the airfield. His head was everywhere,
it moved past my bones and entered me. He laughed when we kissed.
He tried to make his way past my boots and leg warmers and socks
and Danskin tights and cotton panties. "I like the layered look, but
this is ridiculous," he said. I helped him get through the barriers I
had constructed. I knew, without a doubt, I would love him as much
as I have loved anyone, because I could see the child in him, and the
excitement of a parade, and I could also see the soldier in him. He
was, in many ways, like the heroes in my mysteries: tough but also
childlike. He was unafraid of death, with a secret side that he decided
to show to me in a truck in the woods. Outside the truck, frogs cried
out in the mud.

Over the next three months we never tired of touching. When
he had to go *into the field,* which was how they described a week in
the woods practicing war, he had to parachute back onto the airfield
midway between my apartment and downtown. I rode my bike the
nine miles around the lake whenever I could and sometimes I saw

dozens of chutes opening like mushrooms raining from the clouds. Then I raced home knowing that as soon as he was dismissed from formation he would knock on my door and we would be rolling and kissing and I would remember why I loved him. Over those months I also learned many things about him: his mother was an alcoholic who stabbed him when he was nine and set the house on fire when he was eleven. He pulled her away from a flaming couch and saved her. His father was a colonel in the air force who was gone most of the time when he was born, and he and his mother lived in Japan when his father was serving in Vietnam. Mike's first mother was a Japanese nanny who treated him like a flower while his mother was at cocktail parties. One night he told me about his memory of being taken from her at the airport when his father was reassigned to the States. He was five and as he described watching her fade away down the walkway, he started crying. I rubbed the edges of his shaved head, and his thighs were as wide and as lovely as birch trees. I leaned against them and looked up at the sky.

I didn't know what to do with myself at work. Eye, ear, nose, and throat meant cataract surgeries and sinus surgeries and the occasional chemical peel. The patients slept through the night and I hung some antibiotics or helped a few people to the bathroom, but the eight hours felt like sixteen. I wanted to be *necessary*. Anne, meanwhile, never stopped. Neurology in this private hospital meant strokes and the elderly. All head trauma patients went to the city hospital, so Anne's night was a backbreaking cycle of bed changes and suctioning and turning people from one side to the other. For the first time since we met, we were out of sync on an assignment. I loved Savannah, was *in love* in Savannah, and she was beaten down by the hours, the work, and was missing Randy. She could not imagine signing up again when the third month was over. I had gotten my own apartment, so Mike and I could be alone without worrying about roommates. I was determined to sign up but was going after one of the positions at the city hospital. I was tired of the impermanent life of the traveler. I was spending as much time as possible with Mike. Anne, on the other hand, had monthly phone bills that exceeded six hundred dollars from talking to Randy about their future.

At the end of the third month, I drove Anne to the airport. She and Randy were going to try living together in Austin. I was happy for her, and she was happy for me, but we cried at the gate because we didn't know when we would see each other again. I drove back to my new apartment, which was a studio in a wooded complex with a pool. Mike was lying on a chaise in the sun. I watched him from the entrance before I said hello. His body was perfectly sculpted but short, like a squat baseball catcher. I knew by now I was what people considered fat, my hips large, my arms flabby in sleeveless shirts, but I felt so damn sexy, I wasn't surprised he wanted me. I realized the old dresses had allowed me to hide parts of my body that now I was comfortably displaying. A few times since we met women had approached him when I was in the ladies' room or busy talking to someone else and asked him why he would be with a fat girl like me. Once a girl completely ignored me at a table and came and tried to sit on his lap. When Mike brushed her off and said, "Sorry, I'm with her," and pointed to me, the girl just looked at me, laughed, and said, "Her?" I didn't know why I kept moving into a larger body, but I knew when I was with Mike I felt completely beautiful and wanted the lights on and didn't feel inclined to hide anything. It was draining to deal with all the judgment, and I started to polish anger like an apple. I carried it everywhere I went, and spent less time with women, and more time with Mike and his friends.

When I was in fifth grade, there was a girl in our neighborhood who was a year older than me. She was the self-proclaimed leader of the group of girls who lived in the blocks around me. When Ellen, who carried a broom around that she named *Genghis Khan,* proclaimed during the first week of fifth grade that no one was to talk to me, everyone complied. I spent many days on the stoop after school watching them walk by, laughing, while my brother and his friends played in the street. After a couple of weeks, one of the girls, Lorraine, broke rank and said hello to me. Ellen was enraged and took Lorraine's books and shoes and threw them over the synagogue fence. That sealed it. No one would dare talk to me after that. It was worse than being beaten up by the Puerto Rican girls from PS 2. I was invisible.

My brother decided that I was stupid to care and encouraged me to play with his friends, so I did. The days were suddenly about baseball and high bouncers slammed against the stoop steps and little friendly punches and fake wrestling to the ground. This was how it always was with my brother, he couldn't stand suffering. I don't think we ever really talked about what he was doing, how he was saving me, but he did. For the rest of my life I would meet women who challenged me: "You like men better than women," they'd say, and I would admit there was a little leftover adoration of men from the year boys rescued me from the systematic shunning of girls.

So in Georgia, all those years later, I was twenty-seven years old but once again I found myself shut out, this time by the younger traveling nurses who were running together and giggling when I took my big body to the pool. Mike's friends wanted to be around me and were always asking me questions about women and would say things like, "You're the kind of woman I want to marry and have a family with." Instead of marrying, Mike and I made a little nest of a life that was about me being alone and working when he was in the field and being in a community of men when he came back.

The *Oxford American Dictionary* defines *escape* in a number of ways, and all of them applied to me during the years I spent in Georgia. First, escape means "to get oneself free from confinement or control." The years I spent there, with Mike, were about getting free of the control of my mother. While I had lived away and done other things she didn't approve of, with Mike I felt fully separate from her and from her sexual humility for the first time. *Escape* could also be used to describe a leak of something dangerous or liquid, like gas. My grief had been bottled up and was explosive, and during those years I started to let it leak out of my soul, until it slowly evaporated in the mossy woods where Mike and I hid in my truck, under the planes taking off at Hunter Army Airfield. I thought it was possible that I had found someone who loved me as much as Johnny had, and maybe more important, who *liked* me as much as he had. I felt the same safety with him that I had with my brother. One night when I'd been crying about something, he tried to talk to me about Johnny. "This isn't about my dead brother!" I shouted. I think I even threw something soft at him, a couch pillow or a pair of socks. He held me and braided my hair and we curled up together on the bed and he said something funny and the hole in my heart, which had been shredded with loss, felt like it was actually healing over, like the burn wounds on Frank in New Mexico, and I said, "Holy shit, it is all about my dead brother, isn't it?" Mike laid his heavy legs across mine and I fell into a sleep that was like my childhood sleep before anything bad had ever happened to our family.

According to the dictionary, though, *escape* also means "to succeed in avoiding (capture or punishment)." I was still avoiding the dimension of my spirit, and the punishment I thought I deserved for moving to Virginia all those years ago, when I left my brother waving on the stoop. I tried not to think about it, but it was like barbed wire around my soul. As long as I didn't try to cross over to that time by reliving his image as he died, the barbed knots wouldn't tear at me. But it circled and kept me in one place, kept me from thinking about a family of my own. It kept me wanting to move, not to be too still for too long.

So for almost four years I escaped into Mike's arms, and I escaped into the bodies of patients where my skills were honed. My compassion was a constant reminder that I might be able to undo the sin, the great sin of having abandoned the person I loved the most when he needed me the most. I also escaped sentencing. The two ways I served the body also served each other. The better I got at caring for the damaged body, the less afraid I was of the body's limits in love. Sometimes, with Mike, I felt like I was the man, I found so many ways to enter him, and he was trusting of me, and so he just opened himself more and more.

One Saturday, Peter, a friend of Mike's, took us out on the Savannah River in a little speedboat. Peter was about five years older than I. He was always encouraging us to get married. "You don't find someone like this very often," he said to Mike. "Don't let her go." Mike said, "I'm sure we will, we just don't know when." I sipped a wine cooler and looked out over the dark water. I wouldn't make a good military wife, and we both knew this. I also knew Mike was in it forever. A lifer, just like his father. But it was a beautiful day and I tried just to enjoy the boat ride even as a wide grief split through the center of my back and ended in a burning in my throat. That night we went to a party at the Officers' Club for all the guys who had been in Panama together. Mike said, "Please don't say anything about Reagan to my CO, you'll get me an Article Fifteen." He was talking about the ongoing arguments he and I had about President Reagan, whom I detested and his commanding officer adored. An Article Fifteen was a punishment and I would have laughed except I knew Mike wasn't kidding. I wore all black to the party and the other wives and girl-friends were in little khaki skirts with blouses or flowered dresses with fake lace collars. "Oh, I thought everyone was bringing cookies or cake," one said when I walked in empty handed. I just shrugged.

It was inevitable. After forty-five minutes of quietly listening to patriotic clichés I said something about *Bedtime for Bonzo* and I saw Mike go red and the frown on his CO's face got darker. "You're going to have to learn to control her," I heard him say to Mike. I immediately left. Mike came with me, but I couldn't even speak. There was a moment when I felt guilty for how I had pulled him from the men who meant so much to him. He should have stayed there and let me go alone, but he was trying to be faithful despite his disappointment. He was in his dress uniform with his black beret, but he looked as helpless as a little boy in a flaming house. I went to the driver's side of the truck and saw a couple of his friends watching us. "At least let me drive," he said. And I did.

After my first three-month assignment at the private hospital I was transferred to the city hospital, to the head trauma floor. The world seemed even more precarious there; the simplest mistakes were suddenly magnified into unforgivable outcomes. One night a forty-year-old woman went out with her friends and came home drunk. She sat on the toilet and passed out, falling forward and hitting the top of her head on the bathtub, which faced the toilet. She hit in such a way that she broke her neck, and when her roommate found her, hours later, she was wide awake but paralyzed from the neck down.

Another time a man woke up on my unit after crashing his car. He had broken both legs and bled into his brain, which required a craniotomy with the placement of Jackson-Pratt drains. He woke up in traction with small bulbs extending from a massive dressing on his head. When I explained where he was, he asked, "What happened to my kidney stone?" He said he was getting married in a week and he'd heard we had one of those sound wave machines to break up kidney stones, so when he got the familiar pain, having had kidney stones before that had required surgery, he drove the hour to our hospital to try and avoid missing his wedding. On the way there, he got a spasm, lost control of the car, and ended up in a ditch.

One Saturday a man named Gene went out on the Savannah River with his brother and his wife. Gene's wife was three months pregnant, and they'd just started telling people. His brother had a speedboat and they were enjoying the sun and a few beers, except for the wife, who wouldn't even drink coffee now that they were finally expecting their first child. Midway to Skidaway Island, a jet skier got too close to the boat. Gene's brother overcorrected a turn and tipped Gene into the water. Gene swam one way and his brother turned another. The propeller passed across Gene's face and scalp, taking eight slices before his brother shut off the motor.

In shift report we heard that the brother had nearly fainted when he lifted Gene back into the boat. The left ear was gone, the left eye was gone, and brain matter was poking through the shattered skull. Gene went straight to surgery from the ER and when I took report at midday word was he'd be on our floor in a couple of hours. No one wanted to take him. Everyone knew how hard it would be. Then we heard the wife was in the ER, miscarrying their baby. I finally offered to take him because I was in charge and I knew it was expected of me.

We rigged up a cot in the room for the wife on a suggestion from her OB doc, who thought they needed to be together. She had an IV with just a few fluids and had been given a mild sedative. I took her in the room first and got her settled. She was sleeping when Gene came down from the recovery room. The surgeon had done a beautiful job. Each slice of skin had been reattached like a fan and sewn together with hairlike blue sutures. Despite the severity of the injuries Gene appeared to have lost no neurological function. He was on high-dose IV antibiotics, which was standard with an open head injury, and we needed to watch him for signs of meningitis. His face was completely reconstructed but for the missing eye and ear. The remaining portion of his face was handsome, the unshaved side of his head covered with sun-bleached blond curls. He looked up at me to see how I would react to him, and I looked him squarely in the good eye. The plastic surgeon preferred no dressings on the wound, but we needed to apply very thin layers of antibiotic ointment to the suture line every two hours. I explained this to Gene and reinforced the story of what had happened. I explained the things we needed to watch for: fever, nausea and vomiting, increasing headache. He understood, he said.

The neurosurgeon came about ten minutes later. He said all the same things I did and also told Gene about his wife losing the baby. Up until now, Gene thought she was just there, on the cot, so she could be with him. I realized minutes into the neurosurgeon's visit that the wife had woken up but was pretending to still be asleep. I could tell by the change in her breathing and in the stiffening of her posture. She had fallen asleep facing the wall and she stayed turned like that. I wondered what it would mean for her, to have lost her handsome husband. Now she would be stared at when she was with him. And when they did have a baby who was whole and good looking, would the child be embarrassed by Gene's face? Would he feel shame when his friends met his father?

I made rounds with the doctors and helped the staff feed patients who couldn't feed themselves, then went back to check on Gene. When I walked into the room, he had turned the bright light out and only the small light over the sink was on. In the shadow I could see his IV pole next to the cot. He had given his wife the bed and she was sleeping again, her breathing was soft and deep. He had his good eye turned toward me. I shone a penlight on his face, checked the sutures and the pupil of his remaining eye. The room was full of grief. He took my hand and held it for a minute; in that moment, between us, I could feel the swirling river and sharp propeller in its efficient spin. I could see his blood in the water and the flies skimming over it, his brother's near-faint, his fall backward, then the way he recovered to reach forward into the river, toward Gene. I could see Gene rising now in his brother's arms into the boat, changed forever, and his wife, at the sight of him, letting go of everything, even their baby. "You'll be OK," I told him. "The surgeon did a beautiful job." He squeezed my hand once more. And I left him, as I leave all the suffering, alone in the dark.

When I got home, it was past midnight and Mike was already in bed. I lay facing him and traced his features, which seemed as perfect as a plum, as perfect as a high note blown through a flute into the air between us. The pillow held his vulnerable skull and he faced me and opened his eyes as my hand was about to land on his lips. "Bad night?" he asked. But I couldn't answer him because I was still standing alongside Gene. I just started crying and Mike knew enough not to ask anymore. I shifted closer and my head was level with his mouth and he was kissing me, he was kissing light blue sutures all down the front of me. We were in bed, we were in the water in a boat that could not tip and the propeller was as soft as butter and we were safe as we rocked inside each other.

I Learn Everything in One Day

IN THE SPRING OF MY THIRD YEAR IN SAVANNAH, I AGREED to transfer to the oncology floor for a few months, and on the first night, I met Bernard and his family. Bernard was a sixty-year-old man who was in great shape until he started to have diarrhea every day. He'd been diagnosed with pancreatic cancer, and by the time he came to my unit three months later, he was dying, having failed a few attempts at chemotherapy. His wife was a short, intense redhead who was determined that he wouldn't suffer. He had three children, a daughter and two sons, all grown. The daughter was married and had a new baby. They were all with him. He was a mentor to everyone who entered his room, even me. He was teaching peace and forgiveness and joy. All his lessons came forth from his body, which had been starved by the cancer and from his bones, which were bird-like and fragile. He had IV morphine if he needed it, but he liked to be awake. He no longer had control of his feces and shit poured from his rectum, which was red and swollen against the flat bones. He didn't have enough fat left to have buttocks. The room smelled like a barn, but most of the time I didn't notice it because Bernard's eyes were always exploding with blue happiness at all the family that came and went.

His children decided they wanted to do something special and because I was the nurse he had gotten closest to, they wanted me to be there. They prepared a slide show for him from family photos and they wanted me to be there when he saw it. I told them I could take my dinner hour and do it; otherwise I wouldn't be able to leave my other patients uncovered. They agreed and we picked a time. I brought extra cotton gauzes and ointment and blue plastic Chux, and pain medicine just in case he needed it. I knew the other nurses thought it was a problem that I would spend my dinner break with him.

"You've got to set limits with these people," one nurse said.

"Please," I said. "I hope when I'm dying no one sets limits with me."

They just shook their heads, they were so sure I was wrong. And maybe I was, but I felt like an honored guest. The invitation was like crystal between Bernard and his family and me; it shimmered and it sang.

I will never forget what it meant to be in the room with Bernard and his family as one by one the slides of his life flashed on and off the screen. All the early pictures were in black and white, and in them he was handsome, and his children were laughing, climbing on him, being pulled in a wagon, splashing him from a small pool, while his wife looked on. It was impossible to be removed from the tears in the room, his joy and his grief were rising in the air together. His children caught their breath, and one by one they stood beside him and held his hand. I stood behind him between the wall and his bed. He was turned away from me watching the photos click into place. The entire hour I was there blood oozed from Bernard's rectum. Periodically I wiped it away and applied soothing cream. I rolled up the old Chux and laid a new one, and wiped, and tried to keep him dry and comfortable in the most unobtrusive way. Something was happening to me as well, some split in my heart was widening. The floor felt rubbery. I noticed partway through the slides that Bernard's skin was clammy and I knew the blood loss was taking a toll. I felt his pulse by sliding my hand under his elbow and he reached back and squeezed my fingers. I knew as well as he did that he was inching closer to the time he would die. In the squeeze of my fingers he was saying, let it go, don't let anything interrupt this time. I knew I should take his blood pressure, which would be low, then increase the IV fluids and lay his head flat, but I honored his silent request, and there he was, in an old photo, reading the Sunday paper on a porch swing while his son leapt up to scare him. He was pretending to be frightened, rocking back on the swing, throwing his arms up, but it was clear to me, there was nothing he was afraid of in an ordinary day.

After the slide show was over, I finally did the things I might've done sooner. His pressure *was* dropping, the blood was pouring from him now. I called his doctor and we talked to the family and they all decided, along with Bernard, not to do anything else. When he got cramping pain in his back we increased the morphine and he was fading and it was like the tide going out, an almost unnoticeable retreat, except suddenly the water was gone and the rocks were exposed and against the sand little minnows were jumping. Bernard died peacefully about twenty minutes before I went off shift. I offered to stay and do postmortem care so the night nurses didn't have to. I wanted to spend those last seconds with his body after his family had laid their kisses on his face. After they had packed up his comb and bathrobe and slippers, and after his wife had taken his wedding band off his ring finger and put it on her thumb. I hugged them all good-bye, and I didn't know it then, but they were changing the way I would live my life. They had been teaching me a way to be with my own mother and father, a way to undo the flight to Virginia, to escape the months lost with my brother. Bernard's body, its sharp bones and translucent skin, rose in the lightness of the day, in the successful exit of his soul and his breath.

Bernard and his family made me realize that I wanted back into my own family, or more honestly, to be in it, in some ways, for the first time in my life. I had extricated myself with all my travels and my casual calls home. I was wondering if I was somehow destined to wind up with neither my family nor Mike, and for the rest of my life, I would have only traveling acquaintances and temporary addresses.

Then Mike did an extraordinary thing. He decided to leave the army and move to Warrensburg, Missouri. He got a virus and a fever after walking point in a swamp and while he was on sick leave he suddenly felt he wanted to have a permanent home. And he wanted it to be in Warrensburg, Missouri, where he'd spent a couple of years in high school. Other than Japan, it was the only place he'd ever associated with home. We took a vacation there, stopping in Independence to meet his father. Warrensburg was a small town with missile silos and military men in jeeps riding around the perimeter. It was humid and flat. The crows were plentiful and loud. I told Mike I would live in forty of the fifty states, but Missouri wasn't one of them. Friends said, "You mustn't really love him. If you loved him, you'd go." Was this what was missing in me, I wondered, the ability to sacrifice for someone else?

Mike and I decided to see what would happen. Maybe I would move to Kansas City. Maybe he would come back to Savannah. He needed time to imagine his new life with no obstacle courses, no parachutes, with no brotherhood of combat or rugby. Secretly, he imagined I was happy because I hadn't liked the army life, but he was wrong about that. His passion was suddenly gone. With his hair grown out of its special cut it seemed as though his energy was gone out of him too.

The day he left Savannah I called in sick to work. I watched every last thing: the shorts he chose to wear, the blue striped T-shirt. How could there be a T-shirt that was acceptable for leaving me? He went to the mall and came back with a framed poster he'd gotten for me. It was a black-and-white photo of a dancer holding an infant in his arms. All you could see was the dancer's flat chest and abdomen, his taut upper pelvis through the tights, and the infant, supplicant in his arms. Mike knew I'd wanted this photo; it was a gesture, and I accepted it. When he finally left, he turned, he was always good about turning and waving, and he was just as faithful that day. When I turned away from the door, I noticed a line of ants across a bruised pear in the wood bowl. Next to the bowl, Mike's hand cloth, folded neatly, like he'd been taught to do in the army. I wished it would rain, but it didn't, the sun was a taunting bully through the window. I should've gone to work.

I stayed in Savannah and entered the reeds of my high grassy spirit alone. The weeds closed over me. I had nothing to show for the years since I got in my green Chevy Nova and left my poor brother on the stoop, except for the patients who allowed me into the passion of their deaths, and what kind of life was that? Even the willows took advantage of my dark mood, they hung down across the path as I rode my bike in circles listening to Vivaldi's *Four Seasons,* trying to find a place to be, trying to find a life.

I spent six months alone in Savannah. Mike called every Sunday and updated me on his transition to Warrensburg. He described his apartment in the basement of a house with a field out back. We talked about visiting each other. About all the ways we were still together.

One night my father called to tell me the doctor had found an abdominal aortic aneurysm on a routine x-ray. He was going to need surgery as soon as possible. With Christmas just two weeks away, he'd be scheduled in the new year. I decided right then that I would leave Georgia and go home. I gave notice at work. I sent to New Jersey and New York to renew my nursing licenses there. I was sure this was to be my test, and I wouldn't fail my father like I had failed my brother. I would not run this time, except to run home.

When I was driving north two weeks later there was a dusting of snow. I imagined I would be home for just a year or so. I was not planning beyond that. I couldn't know then that a plague was making its way into the lives of many men, a plague that would become a huge part of my life, that would redefine suffering for me and for my generation, like World War II defined my parents' lives. That day, driving through Virginia, I felt exalted. The snow. The horses. Just six hours to go.

PART III

I Can Only Save Myself

Everyone May Be Lost

I TOOK A TEMPORARY JOB WORKING NIGHTS IN THE EMER-gency room at the hospital down the highway from my parents' apartment, where I lived while I saved money. My father was scheduled to have the aneurysm surgery on January sixth, my birthday. He knew it was a risky procedure and worried that if he died he would ruin my birthday for the rest of my life. I told him not to worry and seven hours after he went into the OR the nurses in ICU settled him in for some close monitoring. When they came to get us in the family room they said he kept mumbling "Happy birthday." We told them it was my birthday and they decided I should see him first, and my mother agreed. He was pale and flat on his back. I touched his arms, heavy with red curls, and against his pale skin his freckles were a dramatic brown. He was smiling. He hadn't died on my birthday, he understood that. And I understood he was the blessing of my life. That I had been gone for almost ten years, and I had been allowed to return and touch him as he wakened. "Happy birthday, Mare," he said.

I hated the ER job. All the drunks and attempted suicides. The knife wounds, the car wrecks. I didn't have time to minister, to practice my sainthood. No time for foot rubs or back rubs or delicate dressing changes. It was all about quickness. Sometimes I would work on someone for an hour and get them up to ICU and then say, "What was that guy's name?"

My mother was delicate and empathetic, but she could also have an edge. I spent most of my life blocking out all her advice and closing my eyes when she tried to make sense of my decisions, but one morning after a bad night in the ER she calmly said to me, "You should go back to the cancer hospital, you were happy in New York." I actually heard her. I would be able to get a hospital-housing apartment in a good neighborhood. When I was with Mike, or exploring the West with Anne, I hadn't been writing at all, but since Mike and I were apart it was something I'd returned to. I realized I wanted to be near my poetry friends and take a workshop or go to readings. I thought, surprisingly, she was right. It would mean I wasn't traveling anymore. It would mean I was going to live in the city, something I never expected to do again. But I felt it. She was right. I decided just to trust the way what she said settled in my bones. In the past six years just mentioning I'd worked in that prestigious hospital had opened doors. I knew almost all my skills were honed there. I made a call.

Three weeks later I had a job offer. Outpatient chemotherapy. I would have to be trained, but it was day shift, every weekend off. The job came with an apartment, and not in the hospital building next door, but five blocks away in a luxury building. I had a L-shaped studio for nine hundred dollars a month, a steal in Manhattan. I was happy on the chemotherapy unit. During the day I would come out and put on a lab coat and rub the cold arms of my patients and put in a needle with such skill that sometimes they waited two hours just for me. I rolled alongside their recliners on my little stool and looked into their eyes. I wasn't afraid to look into their suffering or into their fear, and they knew that, and truthfully, I loved almost all of them. But when I went home it was as though I entered a cave. I would look at the hanger in the closet and look at the coat in my hand and I couldn't bear to hang it up. Instead, I'd drape it on the back of a chair. It was too hard. So I would order a pizza with extra cheese and open some wine and I'd get into my overstuffed chair, where I made a world of salt and wine and bread and disappeared into the TV or the phone or sometimes—and here was a hint of my salvation—into words lined up side by side in a book.

On the chemotherapy unit each nurse was assigned primary care practices so the patients would have some continuity. I had breast cancer and lymphoma patients. We would go up to the double-sided closet outside the pharmacy and look at the shelves full of red bins of medicines and search for our primary care patients. The glitch was that there were always nurses who were further behind than others, or there were practices like head and neck or immunology that didn't have enough patients to have a primary nurse. You could bypass one or two patients to get to your bin, but you couldn't bypass an uncovered practice. I mean to say you shouldn't bypass an uncovered practice for your primary group, but of course, people did all the time. The nurses were split between those who worked really, really hard and those who walked slowly, intent on avoiding the chaos that I and two of my friends operated in all the time, four patients going at once, all day long.

Many things happened to me in that first year on that unit, but the most significant was that I started to pull the immunology bins. I took on those bins so automatically, I couldn't know that what I saw there, or the people I met by that act, would change the direction of my life and bring me peace, but not right away. Initially it would be the hardest thing I'd ever done.

When I was sixteen years old I read *The Plague* and *Jude the Obscure*. I read them more than once because there was something delicious about the darkness. It was then that I started to crave isolation, to crave the world of the word, the sad note, the tragic word. I wanted to carry the weight of the world, and to be heroic.

But I was also saved by the image, by words that aligned themselves for me. Words flew up in my face, and they were extraordinary birds. I was one of the flock. Was I as colorful as I hoped to be? I was. Did I weep when certain words arrived side by side? I did. Did I expect that *The Plague* I studied as a child would become a real story that I would almost get lost in? I did not. I thought it was all about imagining. I thought that people couldn't suffer in those numbers and die at the rate they did. But they did, and worse than the suffering was that once again there were symbolic red Xs on the doors in the form of meal trays undelivered outside hospital rooms. Men who looked sick were shunned on city buses; sometimes another passenger would inch away from the sick one, sometimes they would actually get up and change seats. The streets of New York started to fill with young male skeletons with large purple lesions and diapers and canes and Seeing Eye dogs. What was happening? Wasn't it enough that I still had my brother and the young dying boys from ten years ago in my heart? Weren't they enough to carry?

Until now, until 1987, I thought I had seen some difficult things. I had no idea; the old sadness I could bring to mind was easy in comparison to what I was about to see. I ironed my lab coat and work pants and a bright silk blouse. I wore comfortable shoes and headed to the closet of bins. Someone should've warned me about what was to happen, but no one did, and so foolishly, I announced, "I'm taking an immunology bin. Someone's got to deal with these people."

Imagine a gray box, lined with felt; there is nothing in it except a white stone. Imagine a made bed in a cloister under a solid-brass crucifix, or a feather on the lawn, or imagine instead, a man covered with purple sarcoma lesions in a chair by a window, the light on the outline of his face. The bulging outline of his tumors there. Can you see his hands? They are swollen and gray with barely healed needle sticks from last week's chemotherapy. He moves his head on the back of the recliner, shifts his head just enough to see the river outside. His hair, strands of it, stay on the back of the leather chair. All around me in those days was the image of the singular: an apple on the grass, a tugboat on the river, and those men, sitting, looking out the window rather than at us. Who knew where they stood in the line of dying men? Who would be gone by next week? There were days when no one could bear to look around the room.

Although there were moments of a singular suffering unlike anything I had ever seen, there was also, at one time, a room where everyone came together to do hour-long respiratory treatments to prevent Pneumocystis carinii pneumonia, and in this room, there were chaos and laughter, in this room, hope. Surely the mere numbers of the men there meant we would be able to save them. They couldn't all die, could they? This many men?

Oh, but they did. The room emptied and filled, emptied and filled, until there were women there as well; until the National Institutes of Health or the Public Health Department or someone decided that all these people together in a room were presenting a health risk to the staff and to each other, and they resumed the posture of the crab apple, of the feather, of the gray flannel box. There was beauty in the tragedy, and humor.

There was a stunning man, Howard, from Israel. He had solid arms and a dancer's waist. His eyes were always filling with tears, and he spoke openly about how terrified he was. He would sit in the waiting room and look at the other men around him, and picture himself, he said, becoming one of them. We reassured him that because his immune system was as strong as anyone's we'd ever seen, surely by the time he needed medicines we would have more options. I can remember the feel of his skin under my hand the last time I drew his blood. Sometimes when I am holding a child's hand I remember how soft Howard's arm was. I mentioned it to him once. "Well, I've always taken really good care of myself," he said.

Three days after his appointment, Howard's mother contacted the doctor to thank him, and to thank all of us. Howard had checked himself into a hotel room and killed himself. His mother told us about a note he left on the hotel door addressed to the police. "I'm HIV positive," it said. "Please be careful."

In those days we kept African violets in the staff bathroom. I remember laying my head on a stack of paper towels and looking into a violet's eye. I rubbed my own hand over my left forearm, trying to remember the feel of Howard's skin, and it worked, he was there before me, and I had a chance to say something that raised the fear from him, raised it from his spine where it was tearing his bones to shreds. I said something magical and profound, and he left this time, with his solid body and his tenderness, and he didn't want to die.

There was more than one suicide, despite a lot of support and the laughing room with the respiratory treatments, and our confidence, and all the clinical trials. We could do nothing to stop men from picking up the paper and reading the dozens of obituaries, from reading so many names they knew.

I knew in the early days of the AIDS epidemic that there was a moral issue at stake. I had memories of Camus's book. Didn't the doctor take a risk in caring for the dying? What was the risk? What happened to the doctor? All I can remember are cobblestone streets and dead rats. Was I finally going to be the heroine in the story of my life, or would I make mistakes, handle it all badly? For the first time in many years I thought about Molly Pitcher walking the battlefield, lifting the soldier's head so his parched lips could reach the cool water she carried.

It soon became obvious that there was to be no way to romanticize what was happening. We were in the middle of a storm, of a new world, and it was a suffering world, a world filled with stigma and judgment.

I thought about all the men I'd been with. Those I could name and those I couldn't name. The men who might have also been with men:

the Brazilian sailor, the British sailor, the French sailor. The men who might've been with prostitutes. All of the above. And add Mike to both categories. Had he been with men in the woods in Germany? We'd joked about that. Had he been with prostitutes? I had loved the crazy risks of my sex life; I was proud that I felt as capable as a man when all I wanted was to feel good, and I could separate myself from the emotional aspects of sex. Once I was convinced that it was the only way to live, but now . . . now I was wondering if I should get a blood test, and where.

I felt, I had to admit, a strange excitement about AIDS. All my training, all my experience had led me here, and I was surrounded by the best doctors, the best thinkers in the field. Every day had an urgency to it that could not be sustained, but needed to be sustained. My time away from work was merging with my time at work. Conferences, community meetings, and, most of all, funerals.

It is hard to explain the individual stories once the names are gone, and I have so many more faces than names. It feels like a great betrayal, the way I can call up a hand on mine, or the way someone's veins looked on his arms, the pallor of his lips, but his name is gone. There are also names I remember, but sometimes I am so overwhelmed by the people's absences I am unable to say them.

One Saturday, I went to the Pierpont Morgan Library because there was an exhibit of illuminated manuscripts. I found myself taking in the excess of color and imagined the squirrel hairs dipped in lapis or gold. Was I healing in this room of golden books? Was I breaking open in this room? I went into the room of manuscripts and sheet music under glass and realized I was looking down at Milton's handwriting on a draft page of *Paradise Lost*. All the lost men were held in my heart, their souls like a palpable mass behind my ribs. I stared at Milton's words and I felt their souls shift and lighten, and before I realized I was weeping, I saw drops of tears hit the glass. I wondered if there was an alarm that would go off, a sensor meticulous enough for a tear. I hurried out into the side garden, and there were people there, but I couldn't stop crying. To calm myself I said the names of the men: Marco Delbanian, Scott Hewitt, Joseph Minicucci, Luis Bracero, Dan Hirsch, Joaquin Jordan . . . the names kept coming. I felt as though by speaking them I was lining them up in front of the firing squad. How many of them would be gone when it was all over? It turned out every one of them would die, and die painfully, but that day in the garden their names and their lives were suspended among the miraculous texts.

Years later, I traveled to Ireland, and when I first stood over my great-great-grandfather's grave in Coolnacoppogue in County Waterford and learned about his death during the famine, and the death of his two little girls from pneumonia, it was a blustery but shining day. The marigolds were like little spoons of butter all around us. Bittersweet berries hung over the green day. His son John, my great-grandfather, my grandmother Annie's father, had erected a memorial to the members lost in the famine. Annie's father worked the copper mines along the beach, and I headed out there and stood near the squares of shafts marked off in the reeds on the high dune edge. To the left the rock walls still had the patina of copper. Little wagons with their tiny wheels were undisturbed near the shafts. They went down into the shafts that went below the sea. My family was in the salt in the air, I tasted them. All my other great-grandparents were from other Irish counties: Clare, Galway, Limerick. The blood of Ireland, like the cold green markings in the stone, had given me everything I had: my delicate skin, my wide ankles, squat legs, the good storytelling gene, and maybe, just maybe, the sadness that started to edge its way into me when I was ten.

When I stood there I thought I might have finally learned the lessons of the stone walls. I was to lift one rock at a time, study the shape, then pack it into place. In this way, sadness and grief could be measured. I am placing the dead before you now, reverently, in lines of fences. Behind the stone barriers, a roofless church and the ancient lines of ogham carved into a pillar. Each stroke, a letter. Soon the names would be left in the corner of the church below the high tower. Sheep circled me then; it was turning into a celebration of the sacred, their baaing was a song that took back the hills. This was where the stories began and I left them there, alongside all the sacrifices, alongside the hunger that carried on after the mouths were closed. Hunger for prayer. Hunger for a different ending.

Czeslaw Milosz writes, "What is poetry that does not save nations or people?" I never really understood that line until I started to see the epidemic firsthand, but once I understood its meaning, I accepted words as my river guide, I invited words and the sound of words into my bed. I wrote more and more. Most of the poems wound up in folders marked "Abandoned Poems" or "Failed Poems" because they were too sentimental or too long or too something that made it hard for them to find a place in the world, but they did not abandon me. They did not fail me. They grew in their syllable clothes and danced around my room. The lines were like rows in the vegetable garden, they nourished me. Poetry made a room where I could enter freely and paint the walls and rearrange the furniture, always saying, here, by the light, or here, in the cozy alcove. I took a workshop at the 92nd Street Y with J. D. McClatchy and met every two weeks with my poetry friends and in this way, and only in this way, I stayed tethered to life.

I had studied poetry for over ten years but had no degree of any kind. I took noncredit classes at the New School, at Columbia. I studied fiction as well because I kept writing longer and longer poems and everyone was always telling me to cut this or cut that. My workshop with J. D. McClatchy changed my life. He was smart, elegant in manner, and caustic when he wanted to be. One night he asked about the muse. "I don't believe in the muse," I said. He asked me if I was ever overcome by something when I was writing. "Well, yes," I said. What would you call that, he wanted to know. "Well, I think of it as a kind of . . . wind." There was dead silence in the room. He was the master of the pause. Then he looked around the room and asked the other students, "Does anyone else agree with this person who is so obviously *wrong*?" I loved him for doing that. For calling me out on my careless answer. I was always saying how much poetry meant to me, and yet I had never trained myself to be articulate about my beliefs. "Read the classics," he said, giving me a final look of disappointment.

Years later I met a man at a party who remembered me from that workshop. "I think McClatchy was my favorite teacher of all time," I said. "Really?" the man asked. He tilted his head to the door, as if leaving, then added, "I never wrote again." I needed everything to be hard, at least as hard as the nursing work was. I started fantasizing again about leaving the life I had and having another. I did it first in the simplest way. At clubs after work, or at a party, if someone asked what I did, I said, "I'm a poet." They always challenged me by asking, Where have you been published? I would list the few magazines I'd been published in, but add, "I work as a nurse, but that's not who I *am*." No one understood that I was a poet when I sat with the dying men. Nursing itself was like playing pretend dress-up; the world of calculating doses and preparing medicines was just a disguise that allowed me to live in the immediacy of the epidemic. How could I find a way to just be a poet in the world? That was the question I carried with me everywhere like a pumpkin under my arm. A big, orange question. A face carved out of the question with nothing behind it.

In the decades to come, the gay community's response to the plague in its midst would serve as an example of the power of political and social activism. I remember the first time I saw a Silence=Death button, the pink triangle against black. In the first years of the epidemic it took courage to wear these symbols of solidarity. People were mortally afraid of what was happening, and while on the one hand there was tremendous energy involved in pretending it was only a gay disease, there were also rumors about getting AIDS from mosquitoes, from touching, kissing, sharing a glass, using a towel in someone's home. Men were dying alone and even the undertakers were afraid of their poor dead bodies.

The end of the century was measured by the deaths of the famous, but that's not what my story is about. My story is about the gift I was given when I sat with the ordinary men, and later, with the ordinary women. When I sat with someone who was ravaged on the surface, but who, despite stigma and cruelty, sat with her dignity and let me get close to her suffering. Laid her head on my shoulder and wept. Handed me the phone and asked me to call a parent or a brother or someone after years away from her small town. Calling to say, Yes, I am gay and add Yes, I am dying. Sometimes the call was too late and the family turned the person away, but more often the love and acceptance and grief would explode through the phone and all the separate years fell away, rolled from the den of the fox, rolled out like a new life, like a cub, and joyously flipped in the grass.

Citizens were divided on the bus or the subway by those who wore the red ribbon and those who didn't. Politicians and movie stars had handlers who made sure they didn't forget to pin on the ribbon before speaking in public. People suddenly behaved as though the arrival of AIDS allowed for all their bigotry to be spoken aloud. People actually said things like, "It's a punishment from God." And meant it. I didn't know a lot about gay life; the only gay friend I had was a friend from a poetry group and he was someone I might have had a glass of wine with after class, but that was all. Yet AIDS in New York, well, in the medical community in New York, mandated you take one side or the other. It was simple to me. AIDS wasn't a discussion about morality or perversion or retribution, AIDS was a man in a blue recliner waiting for me to start an IV, waiting for me to slowly push a syringe full of medicine into his vein. AIDS was a man with a purple growth on the back of his throat, on his swollen, painful feet, up and down his legs. I found I waited more and more for the time of the week when these men came down the hall. Even the lymphoma group was changing; AIDS-related lymphoma was another cancer affecting these men, and it was a more complicated disease now since people with AIDS couldn't tolerate the heavy-duty chemotherapy that lymphoma patients were given.

In the spring of 1991 a clinical research nurse named Frank told me he was leaving his position in the Infectious Disease Department and he encouraged me to apply for it. I was getting ready to go on vacation but I sent a letter to the doctor who was chief of Infectious Diseases and said I was interested in Frank's position. The biggest boon of this job would be that I would no longer be in the nursing hierarchy, which I had come to think of as an animal always needing to be fed. A job in ID meant I would answer directly to doctors, an attractive proposition. I continued to prepare for my vacation and got a call the day before I left. Dr. Armstrong wanted to talk to me about the job. I prepared an envelope of poems to copy at the Xerox center to take on vacation, and also took an envelope with copies of my résumé in it. I headed to the interview realizing I hadn't asked Frank any practical questions about his job. What does he really *do?* I wondered.

Dr. Armstrong's office was cluttered. He had a feather under glass, a rare owl, a deadly spider in a see-through box. His office was floor-to-ceiling books and pictures of refugees in the Cambodian camps. I sat across from him at a scratched oak table and shook hands.

"Tell me what you know about the ACTG," he said.

"Is that the medicine?" I asked. It was clear I hadn't done my homework.

"That's the job you're applying for," he said. "The AIDS Clinical Trials Group."

"Oh . . . yes!" I knew that. "Well, I don't really know anything about it, except Frank said I would like it. And be good at it," I added. I was rushing through the interview, distracted by the idea that I was going on vacation the next day. Mike and I were meeting in Kansas City and driving to Colorado. We were still talking every Sunday and still trying to see each other twice a year.

"Do you . . ."—he seemed to be searching for something to say, his disappointment quite evident—". . . have a CV?" he finally asked.

"Yes, yes! I do." I opened the envelope and saw I had brought the poems by mistake. "But it's not this," I said. "These are my poems."

The absurdity of this interview had gotten to both of us. I just started laughing. "I don't know," I said. "I treat the AIDS patients down in chemotherapy, I'm just interested in AIDS, I've always been interested in the historic power of a plague. Even in high school, I read *The Plague* over and over again." This seemed to shift the energy a bit.

"What about *The Peloponnesian War?*" he asked me. And off we went into words, into the hallway of my church where I was repeatedly saved.

Before I left the interview I said, "I met you in 1978. I was in the group that was training for the Cambodian refugee camps. For Aranyaprathat." He didn't remember me individually but we both remembered that just two months before we were to leave for the camps, the Vietnamese attacked the border town we were to live in. "My brother had just died here on pediatrics," I said. "I decided I couldn't put my parents through that. And I was scared myself . . . anyway, I've always wanted to work with you." He was warm when we shook hands again, but I went back to the chemotherapy unit fairly sure I'd blown it.

When I returned from vacation I found out Dr. Armstrong had called me on the chemotherapy unit, which was enough to get me in trouble with the nurse manager. I ignored her little corrective messages and called his office. "He wants to offer you the position," his secretary told me. "Great," I said. "I accept." I might as well have said I accept that my life will be forever changed. That I would find a path in life that would not fail me, but would almost break me. I would take this job that would move me, as on a trolley, along the historic line of the epidemic, and would serve to remind me of blessings and injustices, and change forever how much sadness I could withstand. "What do I have to wear?" is what I actually said, though. "And when do I start?"

The day I started my new job in the Infectious Disease Department, I opened the door to the room that all the clinical nurses shared. The center of the large room was open and there were long tables in a square on the outer rim. The research nurses were spaced at intervals along the table, and when I went in they turned. I immediately locked eyes with one and knew we would be friends. His name was Glennon and there was joy and mischief in his greeting. The other nurses, two young women and one old gray-haired woman, said hello and introduced themselves. I was glad to see my space was next to Glennon. I was told I would be doing the ACTG 155 and 151; one was a cytomegalovirus (CMV) treatment trial and one was a toxoplasmosis prophylaxis trial. CMV is a virus many of us have in our bodies, and toxoplasmosis is a parasite we are exposed to all the time in undercooked meat and in the feces of cats. This was how people really died from AIDS. All the bacteria and viruses that settled in our host body and never bothered us reemerged in the body whose immune system was disappearing and caused blindness or pneumonia or brain lesions. Neither one of my studies was expected to enroll a lot of patients, but the CMV trial in particular was very work intensive. My instructions from Dr. Armstrong were to read the protocols, then meet with the individual doctors involved.

Glennon had the antiretroviral trials, which had high numbers of patients. He had joined the department only a week before I did, and so we decided to slog through all the new information together. The other nurses were already trying to make me nervous about the doctor doing the CMV trial, but I wasn't easily spooked. "I'd never work for him," they took turns saying.

This job had none of the chaos of the chemotherapy unit; we had time for breakfast and for attending in-service education and for department meetings. When the doctors were in clinic we went there as well and drew blood from the patients or helped with pentamidine treatments. Pentamidine was a medicine that was given by nebulizer machines to prevent Pneumocystis carinii pneumonia, the illness that was the first hint that something was killing people. Before AIDS, PCP was usually seen only in cancer patients with suppressed immune systems or in organ transplant recipients who had received medicines to prevent rejection. The pentamidine treatment room was noisy from the machines and there was a cool mist of water and medicine in the room. I liked meeting the patients and saw some of the men I'd given chemotherapy to, but most of the faces were new and I was blown away by the sheer numbers of them. Almost no one was doing OK. That was the story of the epidemic, watching each person fail in his or her own way. What was worse than watching an individual fail was watching the dynamic among them. They got to know each other week after week in clinic, and you could see the alarm on their faces when someone who was sicker than the week before walked into the waiting room.

I only enrolled one man in the CMV trial. He was a perfect candidate and after responding for sixty-five days, he went blind. In the beginning, though, we were hopeful. We spent a lot of time during his daily treatments talking about his life, and I could honestly say I grew to love him. He was one of many. What do you do with a love like that? It can't be spoken of. There were a lot of reasons it wasn't healthy. But so many people were being abandoned, and their fear was as huge and as overpowering as a mountain. And comforting was so simple, it was heartbreaking. Love was a tissue, it was an origami bird, it was perfection, it was a call to an undertaker, it was a diaper on a grown man, it was terror when the breath cut off, it was bones, all bones under the skin. The bones grew longer and sharper until the face caved in and the eyes opened and in the eyes the spirit went swirling away in a room with a thin blanket and a half-light. I challenge you. Be there and tell me you could not love the body when it was carrying the spirit away.

I took care of a man whose name was Gernot. He had the elastic band body of a dancer in a Matisse painting. I can still see him in his black pants and black nylon tops, wearing thin-framed glasses that made his eyes look larger. Gernot's face had the angles and grace of the Chrysler Building. Body of light movements. He reminded me of a great blue heron I had seen one summer on the water on Cape Cod. My friend Wendy said I was able to see it because the shadow on the water was so much darker than the bird. The same was true of Gernot. He perched on the edge of a rock looking for sustenance, but his shadow was darker than he was, his shadow was already *in* the water. He was reserved, polite, taut. He came in one day and said, casually, "I am seeing some spots." We knew he had fewer than ten T cells. T cells were the way we measured immunity. Healthy immune systems might easily have a thousand T cells or more. T cells under two hundred meant a patient had AIDS and was susceptible to many infections. Ten T cells meant the normal bacteria in a person's body could easily kill him. We knew Gernot might have CMV retinitis, and if he did he could be blind in twenty-four hours. "Get him to Cornell," the doctor told me. Weill Cornell Medical College was attached to our hospital by a tunnel that was dark and filthy, and whenever possible we took someone outside and across the street, but it was February and sleeting. The ophthalmologist was ready, so I got Gernot in a wheelchair and we raced through the tunnel. Above us were thick pipes and flecks of paint. Some of the lightbulbs were blown out and we made turns that took us up a steep incline, or else we were sliding downhill while I tried to hold on to the wheel-chair. Suddenly, Gernot shouted, "Stop!" I pulled him back and went around to him in the gloom.

"Look," he said, in his faint German accent. "My life has become a Kafka movie."

I agreed. "In the Broadway version," I said, "dancers dressed as retinas would come from behind the pipes." We laughed and I was determined not to move on until he was ready. Finally he nodded at me. "We can go now," he said. He laid his right hand back over his shoulder so that it was just touching mine on the handle of the wheelchair. I wish I could've taken him outside, so that his last moments before knowing would've been about the silver slap of ice and the shine of bare trees along the river.

Gernot did have CMV retinitis. I enrolled him in my research trial, and he was admitted to the hospital for the first fifteen days of intravenous therapy. The researcher, Dr. Polsky, had stayed late. I liked how serious and formal he was. He said to me, "You realize the trial has a twenty-four-hour PK component?" This meant that blood levels of the drug needed to be drawn frequently in the first day. On this study it was every hour for the first twelve, then every two hours for the second twelve. I knew Glennon or the other nurses would help me get the bloods during the day, but there was no one I trusted to draw them during the night. I knew Dr. Polsky expected me to say I would ask the floor nurses or the IV team to cover the night, but when he said, "Who will do them?" and I answered, "I will, of course," I knew we had found our common ground.

Gernot looked even thinner in his hospital gown. His glasses were the only thing on the bedside table. I was reminded of the billboard with the large, disembodied eyes in *The Great Gatsby*. Is God as cold as this? Is he just watching this man tonight while his eyesight slowly crumbles? Well, and why not, I thought. In this same building, my brother, and all the young boys, Tony, the baker with leukemia, and Jack, the boy with testicular cancer, had died in rooms side by side. Behind every door in the curve in the bed was a body fighting for its life. A head turned to the window, a woman adjusting a wig, a slipper falling off a foot, a mouth on fire with sores from the medicine, a retch, a head bent over a basin. The glasses, poignantly folded. Gernot's pupils, the dark circles at the center of the eye, were still wide open from the eye exam. Like the black nylon dancer's clothes he wore, his *self* seemed to be dancing away.

I pulled a recliner next to Gernot's bed and set a small alarm clock for every hour through that first night. The only light came from the bathroom, the door left ajar. Gernot was in a private room even though he wasn't contagious. The cancer patients were fragile and he could have had other undiagnosed infections. The room did bring him privacy, even if the privacy sometimes felt like a contagion mark had been cut above the door. That night he told me about his family. He had no one, he said, his parents long dead in Germany, his much older sister living in Brazil. She didn't know about him and he asked me to copy down her contact information. "Not for now," he said. "For after I die." I took it from him and added it to his chart. At four in the morning he woke up and said he was thirsty. I got him a cold juice from the refrigerator and helped him drink from a straw. He wanted to explain why he had no lover. How shame had prevented him from having a lover. He described going to the bathhouses and lying on a cot in one of the little changing stalls and doing coke and getting fucked in the ass repeatedly by different men. He said, "I never even looked at them. I couldn't look at them."

I fell asleep for the final hour of the night. I didn't dream, but there was a boat on the river and I saw it slide between the hospital and the buildings in Queens across the river. It had been a long time since earlier in the day when we were gliding through the tunnel between here and there. Gernot was right, we were in a Kafka novel. Where was the jury? Where was the castle?

After Gernot finished his fifteen days in the hospital he went home with a referral for a high-tech home care nurse. He needed to have his IV treatment every day, indefinitely. The treatment resulted in severe anemia and about once a week Gernot needed a blood transfusion. On those days we tried to organize his treatment in the hospital because he would be there all day. The treatment also made him nauseous and so he was unbearably thin after just two months. His clothes hung on his bones and he had red spots on the skin over his elbows where they poked through like stunted wings. His kidneys began to fail him. We had to keep adjusting his medicines. One day he brought in a phone number and some papers for me. I was in a small exam room on the first floor waiting for his transfusion to be ready. He wanted me to call a funeral home. He wanted to set aside enough money for cremation and burial. He already had a plot in Brooklyn and he wanted to make all the other arrangements. What about your sister? I asked him. I realized he hadn't mentioned her since that first night in the hospital.

"I have decided I don't want her to know," he said.

"Ever? Even . . . after?" I needed to clarify this for his chart.

"Never. She was very cruel to me when I was young, and I've decided I don't want her to know anything about me." He began to describe a piano, and he described himself as a small boy, both parents dead, the older sister taking care of him. He described sitting with her at the piano and being forced to wear a dress, and eventually I realized he was telling me a story in a Rainer Maria Rilke poem.

I talked to him for the hundredth time about meeting with our psychiatrist, just to help him process what was happening. "I'm not crazy, I'm dying," he said, with an edge. He shoved the papers toward me. "This is what I need help with," he told me. We called seven funeral homes before we found one that would talk to us about arrangements. Gernot wanted to be cremated to avoid the cost of a coffin, but we found out that you still had to buy a coffin even if you were cremated. The absurdity of the conversation actually began to lighten his mood. "Can I just have myself sent to you in a shoe box?" He laughed. Then, he said, "I don't know, throw me in the river . . ." I wanted this settled for him. Finally, we found a man who agreed to do the whole thing for five hundred dollars. There would be no memorial service. He agreed to send paperwork to Gernot and I promised I'd make sure everything would be documented in his hospital chart and with the home care nurses. He let out a deep sigh. I tried to remember the line in the Rilke poem, something like *hands over the piano keys like horses plowing through deep drifts of snow*. We had been plowing, he and I, turning up the earth together, asking for someone to help us lay him down, and we found it, and then we just sat, because there was nothing unfinished between us. The sink gleamed its cleanliness, the paper towels were stacked in the corner, and the big red biohazard box reminded us there was an enemy in the room, an enemy even of the clock, for it distorted time and the honesty of time. "Let's go get you some blood," I said.

When Mike was in Missouri and I was back in New York, we took turns visiting each other. At first the noise of my anger about his living so far away drowned out everything he said. Over time the sight of him in his pale blue jeans released me back into his arms, which were softer than when he was a soldier. He was a hard curve of comfort around my waist when we slept facing the grassy backyard, where he had a shed with planks missing in its side. During my second visit to Missouri, I slept looking out at the moonlight on the slats. I could see tiny flying insects in the air, and hear him breathing. Was he the one? Would my life, after all, work out? Hard nudging at my backside, in my sweaty crack, in the humid spring, and we would make love again, not having found a way to be together, not having found a way to be apart.

In 1991, just when I was starting in Infectious Diseases, and meeting Glennon and learning about AIDS research, Mike came to New York. It had been six years of visits and phone calls and the occasional letter. I was with no one else, he was with no one else. He came down the hallway in my apartment building and once again, I felt the inexplicable arc of light between us. He said, you look great, and held me to him and I felt unnerved. We sat facing each other on the couch, and his foot played under my skirt, which had translucent beads hand-sewn in the shape of moons. We made love and he offered up the exquisite promise I had waited six years to hear: "How about I move to New York in September?" It was March, and outside the balcony's glass was crisscrossed with ice; I felt the promise of balance coming back to the bed, I felt the relief of his face reappearing in my life. I knew it would be there after work, the face that would open again and again to take in the stories. I wouldn't have to carry anything alone, I would be able to lay the sadness on the bed between us and he would move forward and face me and kiss me until the sweat and excess of our skin would push the heartbreak out of the bed where it would roll across the rug and off the balcony and into the gray East River.

We made plans. We went to the Village and bought a foot spa and soaked each other's feet and cooked meat loaf because it was the ordinary day that still held redemption. We had kept a shared storage space in Georgia for all those years because we occasionally talked about moving back there together. We agreed that I would drive down to Georgia with a friend over Memorial Day weekend and clear out our things. He held my hand when he talked to me. Behind him, a lemon in the bowl was the sun on a beach, was a tulip in the window, was the most colorful, satisfying thing in all of New York because I saw it while he touched me and I could almost smell its citrus excitement in the clay of the brown bowl, in the lemony happiness that moved into my apartment in New York. September. Month of apples and hurricanes and back to school and big issues of fashion magazines and leaves, turning their tremulous red and yellow bodies. Death of the leaf that started at the edges and exploded into a kind of flower, a lightening of the self, until they fell and flew down the highway under the tires of speeding cars, into the bushes and onto the lawns and even into our hair. Mike would be living here in seven months. He would be facing me on the couch and not going home, he would finally *be* home.

Everyone warned me to be careful in my happiness. I went to the Morgan Library and looked at drawings from *The Little Prince*: the first sketch of the snake with the elephant inside. This was what I felt like: stretched to the limit with the idea of a new shape. I drew an outline of my own fantasy on a paper napkin; it was in the shape of a lily with arrows flying from the center. I took off the Thursday and Friday before Memorial Day and got my car serviced. I told my parents about my happiness.

"I didn't even date soldiers during World War Two!" my mother said.

"He's not a soldier anymore," I said.

"Talk to your father," she said.

Nothing could undo the luxurious feeling I had for everything in the city as I waited for Mike to come.

The paper mill in Savannah lent a certain smell to the whole town, and sometimes, depending on the humidity and the hot wind, you could even smell it as you approached the river on the South Carolina side. As I pulled into town, the scent of wet paper reminded me of everything about Mike, of our first meeting on the dance floor, of our first night making love in my truck in the woods at Hunter Army Airfield. When I opened our storage locker, his old camouflage pants were folded in a box, some papers were in a leather folder: letters from me, pictures of us. I packed up my things, then boxed his belongings and mailed them to Missouri. I almost called him, but decided to hit the beach on Tybee Island, to show my friend Nancy, who had driven down with me, the sights.

In keeping with the purpose of our road trip, I talked nonstop about Mike and the quirkiness of our relationship. The political arguments, his difficult childhood. At the beach I sat in the grassy dunes above the water and remembered how he would bring his military history books there and read long chapters of maneuvers and victory while we lay side by side in the sand. Nancy said she looked forward to meeting him.

When sadness lifts you can't believe you lived under the blanket of it for so long. But while it's there it starts to feel like a regular life, you don't notice it, you stop feeling how heavy it is. The children in the park looked frivolous. Once sadness is gone, you can't stop seeing other people's happiness: a kite over the water, a couple kissing on a bench, the ordinary explosion of color at the vegetable truck. The way sugarcane, with its delicate yellow, rises to the sky. This was the moment I was living in, imagining my own story, and keeping out the sad stories of others.

On the drive home I pulled into a rest stop, and Nancy went to the bathroom. I tilted the seat back on the driver's side, and opened the sunroof, and slept solidly for five minutes, warm May air on my face. It was the last moment I remember before everything changed.

It was impossible to park on the streets of New York, so Nancy agreed to wait in the car at a fire hydrant while I ran upstairs with some things. I planned on making two more trips to unload the car. Then I could take the car to the garage six blocks away.

When I entered my apartment, mail in my hand, duffel bag in my hand, I noticed the blinking light of the answering machine. I noted the number of messages: eleven. Eleven. Eleven. The two red lines of the number eleven, like exclamation points. I hit the play button, and halfway through the first message I sat down in the hard-backed chair my father made for me when I came home from Virginia. All the messages except for two were from Mike's father. Mike, his truck, a tree, his beautiful skull. Mike. His life, hanging. Mike, his mind, his speech, the flaccid arms. His father was leading me through the weekend, explaining on each message the lack of progress, the worsening, then the life maybe not being over, although the life of the mind was over, yes, the memory of everyone seemed to have been left in the bark of the tree.

While I was lying in the dunes thinking about us, Mike was turning and turning over in the cab of his Mazda pickup and forgetting everything, even how to walk, even how to lift his index finger in the air on command. Was he still breathing? Not on his own. Was he moving? Only when two orderlies came and turned his substantial body from side to side. I forgot about Nancy in the car and she buzzed the bell. "OK, OK," I shouted through the intercom. But I wondered if anything would ever be OK again.

Other than the first long conversation with Mike's father, the thing I remember most about those days after the accident was a call I made to the brain injury hotline. I had worked neurotrauma, but I wanted a new knowledge, one that would let me reinterpret the bad news I was getting from Missouri. I had a piece of paper in my hand that had all the technical words for the brain bleed and the fractured bones, and I read them to a man named Bruce at the hotline. Bruce was a nurse who had worked in a neuro intensive care unit somewhere, and midway through our talk I realized what I had known from the beginning, that Mike was gone. That he would spend the rest of his life in a nursing home, until he got pneumonia or a kidney infection, and then, dear sweet boy with the soldier body and the skipping rabbit heart, would die.

For months I spoke every Sunday with Mike's father. For months after that we spoke once a month. The news never got better. Eventually, Mike was moved to a veterans' nursing home in Iowa, and his father, almost eighty years old, moved there to be closer to him. Is Mike alive? In my mind he is, but I cannot find his name on the Internet, and I can't find a listing for his father in Iowa. I can't find an obituary for either one, and while I have Mike's Social Security number, and it would take just $39.95 to *People Finders* to know for sure, I prefer to leave him, unclaimed, out there. My decision is not satisfying, I know, and it torments those who are closest to me. I think I felt that in the middle of so much death, not knowing meant there was hope that one day I'd be in a Home Depot in some town and a boy would turn in an orange apron holding a geranium and it would be Mike and I would say, "I thought you died." And he would shake his head and I would be able to move toward him holding the flower.

What does it mean if he is dead? What would be different about our time together and his willingness to take on all the sadness I carried home from the hospital? I don't want to know if his muscles are contracted in a nursing home bed in Iowa. I don't want to know if he has bedsores. I'm sorry if that is frustrating, but it is significant to me that I don't need to know. It means for once I have chosen not to let death own a memory of someone I love. I have stubbornly told the story about this man I loved as much as my brother, a man who, more important maybe, loved me as much as Johnny did. When I tell someone about Mike and I get to the place where I cannot sum up what happens to him, I feel their incredulousness. But it is how I have chosen to keep it. What does that say about me? That once, years ago, we parted at the elevator for what we thought would be six months. Our kiss was gold and illuminated with the idea of *later*. That was how I wish to leave it: a happiness floating on the nineteenth floor, floating in the little *ding* the elevator made as its doors closed on his face. As he blew a kiss to me, and I imitated a TV commercial popular in those days, catching the kiss like a slap on my face. He had a little wave, not a soldier's wave, there they go, his fingers waving in the air between us, between the closing doors.

The World Is Broken

IN THE EARLY DAYS OF MY WORK WITH PEOPLE WITH AIDS all my knowledge of boundaries exploded. I had never been to a patient's home before unless I was working private duty. I had never been friends with patients until now, and I accepted how dangerous breaking the rules could be. The first line I crossed was in my friendship with Glennon. Within two months he told me he had HIV. We were in the break room and he just said it. We were talking about another worker who had also disclosed his status. It had never dawned on me that Glennon was sick. He told me about his brother Denny who'd died of AIDS four years earlier. Glennon looked as healthy as a horse and was on one of the clinical trials we were doing. I wouldn't have known from Glennon's appearance or attitude, but once I did know, I agreed to draw his blood for him whenever he needed it done. I understood his compassion with the patients, and had new confidence in what he knew about side effects and how the patients felt. In the same way my brother taught me how to be with young boys with cancer, Glennon taught me how to be in this illness, and I was studying carefully, reverently.

In their late sixties, my parents began reading the obituaries obsessively. In the early 1990s, I started my day the same way. When someone died I moved his file from one cabinet to the other. I put a colored sticky dot on his case report form, the research book that held all his lab results, all his blood work. In those days, the files in the *dead drawer* were growing at a fast rate. We kept needing to buy new metal cabinets with secure locks and fireproofing. There was still so much

133

we didn't know, but we realized that one day we might find the answers in those files.

One night Glennon asked me if I would go to the Bronx with
him after work to visit his friend Peter, who was dying of AIDS. Peter
had a brother, Robert, who had AIDS as well. Robert was on one of
the Kaposi's sarcoma studies in our clinic. Kaposi's sarcoma was the
cause of the purplish lesions that at the time were seen on thin men
all over town. The growths were on their hands and legs and stomachs and faces. They were also inside them, blocking their intestines,
making throats close over, destroying livers and stomachs. The tumors
blocked lymph nodes so that arms and legs swelled grotesquely. When
Glennon told me about Peter and Robert I was floored imagining
their parents, their sisters, and wondered how they would survive losing two sons. At this time, there was no other way to look at it. No
one was surviving. I said yes to Glennon and we went to the Bronx to
meet his friend.

The family lived right near the zoo. When we got to their house,
it was already dark, and the winter's chill was in the stones along the
front gate. The chill was on the stoop steps as we made our way
to the door. When Peter's mother answered the door her breath was
white in the air, like smoke released from the Vatican when a new
pope is named. The house was a mix of Irish and Italian Catholic:
a crucifix on the wall with a piece of palm fanned out behind it, a
Christmas tablecloth with appliquéd poinsettias on the border. The
scent of garlic and warm toast drifted from the kitchen. Glennon
introduced me, and it occurred to me that until this moment they
didn't know I would be coming, or who I was. The sisters and the
mother locked onto Glennon, locked onto his seeming good health.
They knew his HIV status and he looked *good*. Were they thinking
that maybe their brothers, maybe the sons they loved could look like
this, too?

I said I should wait in the living room and give them a chance
to visit with Peter, who was in a hospital bed upstairs. But no, but

no, they ushered me with them. As I got closer to Peter's room there was the faint ammonia smell that comes from urinals and urine having to sit until emptied. I smelled diluted bleach and flat flowery air freshener, and maybe, yes, baby powder coming from the room where Peter was dying. I entered the room behind Glennon and saw Peter's face slide into happiness. There was a moment of puzzlement when he saw me, but quickly then, as Glennon introduced me, happiness at a new visitor, brief respite from his thoughts in his hospital bed next to the small window above the zoo.

After a few minutes of polite talk it was clear that Peter's mother and sisters had saved up questions for Glennon and they pulled him out of the room, telling me sit, sit, in the rocker next to Peter. I did as I was told. How could anyone do anything else in the presence of Peter and his suffering body? Peter tried to shrug as if to say nothing was new, the way people come and go and ask questions outside his room. So I sat in the rocker, and I instinctively took his hand, and in the way it always is with the dying, he expressed no hesitation or shyness and he gave his own hand over to me.

Peter's body was celebrated in pictures over his bed: men, shirtless, in the summer, crowded into the back of a convertible by a beach. Peter in an Irish knit sweater standing next to his mother. His face was beautiful and his eyes were a green brown under wavy brown hair. In another, he and his brother Robert were arm in arm and suddenly I knew exactly who his brother was and I knew how sick he was as well. He probably had no more than six months to live.

I am always amazed at the way bones look in a dying body. They are so hard, the skeleton feels like the enemy as it tries to hold the shape of the person in place, but the body sinks against the bones, like earth, collapsing down around tree roots. It is the hands and feet and eyes that go last. I asked Peter if he would like me to massage his feet and he said yes. I went down to the bottom of his bed and warmed lotion in my hands, then rubbed his feet gently from the arch down, centering on the bottom of the sole. We looked at each other.

Glennon had told him I was a nurse and he knew I wasn't afraid of what was happening. That was all the history we needed together. He looked at me and tears fell down his cheek to his pillow. In the hallway, we heard his mother's voice. After I finished with his feet, he closed his eyes and I took a tissue to wipe the tears from his face. I ran my hand over his hair, shifted it off his forehead, and he started to fall asleep. I saw his ribs rise under the sheet. I said a little prayer for a long sleep. I asked his bones to give up their sharp argument.

Glennon was funny, there was no doubt about it, and I heard Peter's mother and sisters laughing. I looked up, he signaled me out of the room when he saw Peter was sleeping, and I understood why he had asked me to come. There was so much to do, so much Peter's family needed to say, so much they would want to ask, and Glennon knew I could spend those moments with Peter so he wouldn't have to be alone. I hugged his mother good-bye. "Do you know Robert?" she asked, meaning the other sick son. "I do," I said, and hugged her once more. Glennon and I walked a couple of blocks to where we could get a taxi. "Honey, we are getting a drink," he said.

We took a cab to Greenwich Village and got wine and pasta in a restaurant before we headed home. "I knew you would love Peter," he said. We didn't say much more about it. I watched the people walking by on Christopher Street and so did he. We were exhausted from the day, and it was a clinic day tomorrow. I knew it was dangerous to get personally involved outside work, the grief on the job was already huge, and to underscore just how dangerous, an ambulance swept by, squeezing uncooperative traffic to the edge outside the restaurant window. There was a siren. There was an alarm. What was happening was faster than the people racing by in the cold. There was no time to think. There was a beautiful man dying above the zoo. Across the street from the restaurant, a Korean grocer tried to cover hundreds of out-of-season tulips in the cold. Their beautiful pink and yellow bodies were falling over in their tall silver buckets. An apple rolled off the cart and disappeared behind a car. How would any of the beautiful men survive?

Glennon became an ambassador, a translator. I moved in and out of lives in crisis and my place was poorly defined. There was a terrible energy to what was happening. If you were seeing it happen every day like we were, if you knew the tender men who were disfigured or dying, it was hard to have patience for anything outside AIDS. I couldn't bear the thought of going to a wedding or a baby shower; I felt I didn't belong in that world, and yet, I didn't belong in Glennon's world either, though I tried sometimes to feel the communion that was there for him. I tried to find a seamlessness between the work and the life, but I was outside both the gay community and the straight community. Poetry floated outside with me, patiently in the air. I didn't recognize what was offered there, but I went to it, instinctively, like someone in a burning building who runs to the exit and finds the world intact even though everything behind them is disappearing. What of Glennon? He was holding open the door of the burning house. He was half in, half out, a silhouette, lit up by the flames. He was frozen in the light by the screams of the dying.

Refuge

~

DURING THE DAYS I WORKED IN AIDS, THERE WAS A GROUP of women who supported my life like heavy beams in a house. They were women I met in 1977 right after my brother died, in the first Jean Valentine workshop I took at the 92nd Street Y. All the years of traveling we had stayed in touch with rare letters or cards at the holidays. When I first moved back to New York I rejoined the group, which had continued to meet every two weeks during all my years away. I need to name them: Wendy, Myra, Priscilla, Lee, Sabra, and Vicki. There was something about these six women in the harder years of my life, their consistency, their good humor. I could get in a boat with them and stop rowing and they would willingly take up the oars and cut the water in rhythm while we glided across the surface together.

Priscilla's mother-in-law, Sally, had a house on Fishers Island, and she let us use it for a poetry retreat every year. The first year I went was 1986. Fishers Island is off the coast of New London, Connecticut, between Montauk Point, Long Island, and Block Island, Rhode Island. I am always as peaceful there as I can imagine being on this earth. The island was not set up for tourists, and that was no accident. The wealthy had their houses there. They had their own golf course and private access to beaches. There was no hotel, just a few rooms for rent in the Pequod Inn. It was the kind of place I was both morally opposed to and grateful to have access to. Every September it was where I gathered strength for the year to come. It was my New Year's Eve, my pilgrimage. I dipped in the ocean there and it had the miraculous healing of the water at Lourdes. I learned many lessons there, and it was where poetry reasserted itself as the saving grace in my life. I understood everything by using my words, or the words of the other women, or by taking on the words we read to one another: Shakespeare, Mary Oliver, Alan Dugan.

The house was on a hill over Chocomount Cove and large enough so that each person had her own room and bathroom. We banished the phone and TV and settled into five days of working on poems and cooking together. When we ate at the long table with the hand-painted dining room chairs we challenged each other's prejudices and made each other laugh until someone had to leave the table just to catch her breath. The days were full of the fellowship of women. No one treated me as lovingly as these women did. Our friendships existed in the way they did because they traveled through poetry, and poetry was what we lay down with each night. We made love to the line and the line break; we held the image in our arms all night while outside the waves crashed and the cormorants stood as if crucified on the rocks, drying their wings.

In the early nineties I started bringing my grief to them and to Fishers Island. Five days was not enough time to unload the bodies I carried in my chest. Five days was barely enough time to name the men and to lay them at the feet of the oyster catcher's thin red legs. The names were picked apart there, but their bodies were still in my arms.

It was part of our pilgrimage on Fishers Island to go to the local museum, a gray split-level with nests and eggs and preserved birds of all sizes. There were re-creations of Indian campsites and pictures of old sailors and their vessels. Mr. Horning, the elderly curator, opened the building for us if we called, for our retreat was always at the end of the summer season. One day he gave us a tip, knowing Wendy was a bird-watcher. "Head out to Race Point," he said. In previous years he had sent us to a dying pond where a great heron had taken up residence among the ducks and turtles, so we did not question him but picked the time we would go to the Point.

Beyond the fastidious lawns of the houses, Fishers was wild. The shrubbery was overgrown on the roads that curved around the island. To get to Race Point we had to drive back in the direction of the ferry on the other side of the island and then cut across a small airfield, driving for a minute or two on the actual runway. In a car you could cross it in under a minute, but it was still frightening when you'd hear the drone of a small plane coming or going as we made a run for it. Once on the other side you could only go so far before you had to get out and walk because the road was rocky and the wind and water had worn big holes in the sand. On this particular day, in 1992, Wendy and I decided to go out alone. We were in her blue Honda with the sunroof open, and just on the other side of the airfield we were unexpectedly in a swarm of locusts. They were in the car and on the hood and leaping in and out the windows, and behind them and above them in their own swooping was a flock of kestrel hawks. A hawk hovered over the sunroof, took a locust with its claw, and put it in his mouth. We locked the car tight and got out to walk into the migration of predators and prey. This was excitement enough for us, but it was just beginning.

The wind was steady and slightly cool. Saltwater settled on our tongues and our hair thickened with brine in the wind. Fishermen stood off the point in a rush of bluefish jumping in the froth. The sheer number of fish was amazing; the fishermen were laughing out loud. We walked past them and they greeted us. The Point had come to life. Out on the ocean the old lighthouse looked like a castle in the water. I felt something let go in my chest, it was the grief of the past few years. I looked at Wendy. She was poised with her binoculars, peacefully watching something off in the goldenrod. "Come with me," she said, and we walked away from the fishermen into the brush. It was only when the first group flew up that I realized we were in the middle of a monarch butterfly migration. The trees and bushes were red with them, feasting and resting. We lay on the ground together and above us the wings languidly opened and closed without flight. Then a hundred or more lifted and floated around us, some landing on us. We could hear their delicate rustle above us. It was the planet at its liveliest. It was a place where the plague didn't exist. There was no death that day that didn't feel necessary. The locust and hawk, the bluefish and the fishermen. We were connected in the life and death, and it all felt vigorous and spiritual. I was joyful in the way children were joyful in play. I reached my hand up and I was in the midst of the monarchs. They flitted and flirted with my hand. My own wings unlatched from my back and my heart beat in time with their wings. Off in the distance the fishermen whooped and hollered. Hawks feasted on the leaf eaters. I didn't know what would happen that year, but I knew I could carry that moment for a long time against the tragedy that would come.

When I first met Wendy in 1978 she was slick and beautiful. She was a *Vogue* pattern with a matching headband and patent leather purse. She smoked and said she drank vodka and got mean, though I don't remember that. I remember feeling uneducated, unattractive, and awkward around her. She had been to Vietnam during the war and her husband was a reporter. They were in their thirties and I was twenty-two. She had what I considered a thrilling life: an apartment in Manhattan, travel to exotic places, a master's from Harvard. When I left for Hawaii in 1980, I would say I barely knew her, though we'd done poetry work together for almost three years. While I was gone I heard that she and her husband divorced and Wendy had been depressed. What I didn't know was that she had thrown herself into self-study with a passion and had developed a new reverence for herself. She stopped smoking, stopped drinking. Wrote a book about Vietnam. She gave up her poised, cold clothes for softer fabrics and pale colors. When I returned to New York it was a different person I met there, and her friendship would change my life.

It could be a silly friendship. She lived twelve blocks away from me in New York, and so we could be spontaneous about getting together. We watched excerpts from the first Menendez brothers' trial. I don't know how we could've believed their defense at first, but we did; it was Shakespearean, we took the stories and the stories within the stories apart. Her brother in California was disgusted with us. "Chair One and Chair Two," he said when he called, showing his preference for the death penalty. We held firm until the second trial, which concentrated on one brother's methodical reloading to finish off the mother. We were sheepish. Wendy's brother gloated.

I benefited from Wendy's work with yoga masters and shamans. She would deliver lessons on letting go of anger or turning over control to someone else or finding my own power. She delivered them in gift packages and demonstrations. One day she said, "Put your hand out" and dropped a dime in my palm. She told me, "Squeeze it as hard as you can, this is what you want more than anything." I squeezed until it hurt. It didn't feel good to grasp so hard. That was the lesson. "Open your hand slowly now," she said. I felt the release all through my body. After that whenever I was wanting something, she'd say, "Don't grasp," and that lesson would come back to me. There were lessons about anger and desire and grief and control, and under them all she accepted the flawed me, the student. We could write poems together in the same room after a while and trigger each other with ideas. Her friendship was as tender as a pink house on a cliff, or a nest with blue eggs.

The same September as the butterfly migration, I went for a walk by myself on the beach. I really wanted to find something I could take back with me. All week I had been looking for a piece of beach glass and couldn't find anything. Now I would settle for a shell, a rock even. I was walking with my head down tracking through brown seaweed when I saw a starfish in the water. It was beautiful and I found myself thinking I could take it out of the water and when it died bleach it in Clorox and take home a gorgeous white star. Of course I had to kill it to have it. I'd like to say it was an easy decision but it wasn't, my desire was crowding out all sense of fairness. I struggled for minutes watching it move slowly in the tide pool. Finally I thought of Wendy. "Don't grasp," I heard her say, and in that instant I knew nothing good would be connected to my taking the starfish. I shook my head, amazed at how stupid and selfish I was even to consider it. I turned to walk back and five feet down the beach I found the most amazing piece of beach glass I have ever seen in my life. It was the palest blue green and had writing etched in it, nothing I could read, but script across it, letters of some kind, and it was as big as a brooch. I raced back to the house to tell Wendy about it. Gifts started to fall around me in those days. After a while, for every tragic loss I was able to find something beautiful. Or was it that the tragedy was helping me see what had always been around me? Or was it Wendy opening me to the world? Whatever it was I was splitting and healing and splitting with the speed of an atom. Did other things happen in the world then? I imagine they did, but not to me. I lived in the five blocks north to my job and the twelve blocks south to Wendy's house. I lived in medicine and poetry, and they were not enemies at all. They celebrated the synchronicity of discovery and hope, of desire and knowledge. I knew there were people all over the world who lived without poetry, but I didn't know how.

A Kind of Miracle

PETER DIED IN THE ROOM OVER THE ZOO IN MARCH, JUST a few months after I met him for the first time. After Glennon called to tell me I went out for a walk and remembered the dying tulips in the Village that first night. I bought two dozen from the grocer and put them in a vase with pennies on the bottom. All week the lemony petals kept their cups upright in the window over the river.

The hardest thing about the wake in the funeral home on Madison Avenue was seeing Peter's brother, Robert. He made jokes about being the next one, but no one was laughing, it was too true. Robert wore a maroon velour jacket and surveyed the room, interrogating the mourners: "Should I be as low as that in my coffin?" he asked. "Did you send those awful flowers?" People were mad at Robert; we thought Peter deserved attention and a reverent respect, but he wasn't getting it. I thought Robert was drunk. I stood next to him for a few moments and saw how thick he had caked makeup over the sarcoma lesions on his face. His family was clustered away from him. I believed he was wishing he had died first. Both boys were beautiful, and for Robert, losing his beauty was another kind of death, and I think he was afraid of how much worse it would get before he actually died. He tipped over and looked into the coffin. "Glennon, honey," he said, "you must promise to do my hair."

My parents tried to be understanding, but they wondered if it was safe to do what I did. I insisted it was. They found it easier to talk to me about people with cancer. Cancer we understood, they thought that work was noble. But this was . . . well, they didn't know what this was. And I was spending too much time with gay men. "You'll never meet anyone if you are always with gay men," my mother said. "I'm not always with gay men," I answered. "I have my poetry friends too."

"You are a strange one, Mare," my father said. "You always have been."

That same year, 1993, I won the New Voices Award for poetry from the West Side Y in New York. I got to do a reading with Richard McCann, who won the Open Voice Award for his poetry collection, *Ghost Letters*. I invited my parents to come. I was always amazed when people told me they couldn't read in front of their parents, or were fearful of them seeing a poem in a publication. It never occurred to me to shield them from my voice. My voice was born in their home, in response to our lives together. Maybe it was a challenge of sorts, to ask them to sit and hear me out, but truth be told, they faithfully came to every reading. Poetry readings were like the best part of our lives together. After so many years of silence, I think they loved that I was talking to them at all, even if it was through poems.

The best thing that happened to me in my relationship with my parents that year was that Tom Hanks made the movie *Philadelphia*. My mother and father were profoundly moved by the film, and it gave us a way to talk about what I saw every day. It shifted the energy between us.

Acquired immune deficiency is a syndrome, not a disease. People died in many different ways, depending on how many opportunistic infections they had, how severe they were, and whether the infections came on top of a cancer diagnosis. I started keeping autopsy reports because I wanted to remind myself of all the ways the body could turn on itself. I knew I would always have the names of the men I'd cared for, but I also needed to keep the unique ways they died, their special suffering. The early autopsies found infections caused by things we carried in us all the time, bacteria from soil, from water, from food, from air; everything in the immune-compromised body was a horrific killer. I had autopsies on my desk that showed toxoplasmosis in the heart sac, CMV in the brain, mycobacterium avium infection in the liver and bone marrow, CMV pneumonia, toxoplasmosis in the brain, CMV in the colon, and more—all in the same poor body. What that translated to, in the person before death, was shortness of breath, profound fatigue, chronic diarrhea up to eighty or ninety times a day, and maybe blindness or dementia. A doctor said to me once, "It's just like cholera, people literally shit their lives away."

Then there were the cancers: Kaposi's sarcoma, AIDS-related lymphoma. The chemotherapy we gave to try to treat the cancer also knocked down what was left of the immune system. Glennon and I would work side by side in clinic, or visit folks who'd been admitted to the hospital. He would find a way to make them laugh, or to leave them hopeful when we headed back to the office.

Our hospital had always been a specialty hospital. We treated cancers by referrals and most of our patients were privately insured, unlike a city hospital that had to accept a variety of insurance types, including Medicaid or even, in some instances, the uninsured. Our financial offices were very reluctant to let us bring people into the institution for care who had no method of payment. It was one thing to see them in clinic and absorb the cost of outpatient visits or lab work, but if that person needed hospitalization, the losses would be crippling. Still, because we received federal funds for research, we were obligated to make some linkages to the less fortunate, and Glennon and I decided to do outreach to a drug rehab clinic in a poor neighborhood in Queens. We offered free counseling and testing and then if the test came back positive we would either offer to see them at our hospital or refer them closer to home.

These were the days when I first understood the epidemic was moving out from the first circle of gay men, into the African American community, and infecting women in that community. Glennon and I gave a lot of positive results to women that year, and surprisingly we weren't asked about treatment or survival when we gave them the news, but almost every woman said, in those first few minutes after being told, "Can I still have children?" We realized this disease we thought we knew so well was now about to change, the faces were changing, the questions were changing, and no matter how we tried to ignore it, in the middle of all of this, Glennon was starting to die.

He put in his request for disability leave and took some sick days, and when his last day of work came, the few of us who knew that he was sick took him out to lunch at an Italian restaurant that had a painted Heaven on the ceiling and angels holding plates of pasta. He wore black dress pants and a short red leather jacket. Afterward, we walked, just the two of us, to the corner of Sixty-fifth and First Avenue and we hugged and then I watched him walk toward Third Avenue. I watched until I could no longer see the spot of red leather between the brownstones on Sixty-fifth Street. I was crying in my lab coat, making my way back to the hospital. I thought about all the patients he had reassured and touched and I thought about him at Peter's wake, and Robert's wake, and how he bent over and leaned into Robert's coffin to comb his hair. I got back just in time for clinic, just in time to see the men lining up. In time to do a quick glance over the faces to see who was sicker this week. Rodney sat in a chair near the waiting room door. He was as thin as a skeleton, with long blond hair. I had encouraged him the week before to try and lie outside on his roof on a chaise, just to get some air. I called him into a room to check his vital signs. He had heliconia across his lap and he raised the flowers toward me.

"Some for you, some for Glennon," he said. Then, "Where is Glennon?"

"Oh, he's not here today," I said, and "Thanks," and "Just sit up here. Did you lie out on your roof?" I asked him.

"I did for a few minutes," he said, "It was nice, but then I looked up, and these black birds were circling . . ." We laughed, like we always did.

Now, at work, I felt completely alone with the sadness. Before Glennon left, we were comrades, and nothing seemed too difficult. Now I could barely stand to make my rounds, and I had to field questions about him, and from some of the clients we'd known a long time. I had to address their fears that he was sick as well. I didn't realize until those days how much I'd depended on being able to walk out of a room with Glennon and into the stairwell, where we would help each other deal with what was happening. Now I left the sickrooms and went into the bright halls and down the stairs to our dark-blue office where I felt Glennon's absence, and carried the story around all day.

Some nights I went to his house and filled him in on what was happening. There was almost never good news, except a few people on the newest clinical trial who seemed to be doing better than expected.

That fall, I applied for a writing fellowship at the Fine Arts Work Center in Provincetown. I also entered eleven other poetry contests. I had a ritual of postcards. I would buy postcards I loved and send them with each entry to be returned to me with *We have received your entry* on the back. Then I would line them up on a ledge I had on my wall, picture side to the wall. When I learned who won I'd turn that postcard around. My consolation would be in seeing a postcard I'd loved again. It was an act of hope for my life. I might be able to leave the epidemic behind. I might be able to forget about it for a while. But in 1994, with just one postcard to go, I didn't seem to be winning anything.

Glennon developed cryptosporidiosis, the infection the doctor had compared to cholera, and in four weeks he lost forty pounds. We had talked once about interventions of all kinds and one of them was a central IV line, a line going into a large vessel in the chest, for nutrition. He was opposed to them, but now we were sitting on his bed, the gorgeous bed he bought at ABC Carpet and Home, a bed worthy of dying in, and we were sitting on an eight-hundred-dollar duvet. "You look sick," I told him. "More than anything you said you didn't want to look sick." He agreed to get the IV line put in and afterward carried bags of nutrition in a little backpack.

When our clinic patients were admitted to the hospital I tried to see them, but sometimes it wasn't possible. If too many people were in the hospital at the same time I could spend half my day visiting. One Thursday, less than a week before Christmas, I tried to get around to everyone since I was taking off Friday and wouldn't be back until after the holidays. We had very few patients in the hospital for the holidays. Phil, the entertainment lawyer, was there with his meticulous crisp pajamas. He'd be going home. Charlotte was in. She was one of our Medicaid patients from Queens and she was in with suspected TB, so she was in a private room. She had been off crack cocaine for three years, but now she was very sick. I admired her for her toughness and we gave it, in banter, back to each other, which was her way of saying thank-you. "Hey, Charlotte," I said, "you know who is in the room next door? The sultan of Brunei!" And we laughed at the ridiculousness of it.

That day I saved Joaquin until last. When I first met him he was one of the most physically beautiful men I'd ever seen, and his decline over the previous two years was frightening. It always was frightening, no matter who it was, but somehow, it scared me more than usual to see his disappearance. He was a mix of Puerto Rican and European heritage. His skin was a luscious light brown, but his eyes were the blue of glaciers. He had salt-and-pepper hair in light curls. I was pretty sure he would die by Christmas.

I knocked. He didn't say anything and so I knocked again. I heard a rustling and went in. He was standing on the top of the headboard of his bed, which was no more than an inch thick. His feet were curved, as in ballet, toward the toes. In his hand was a three-dimensional silver star the size of a dinner plate. His many lines and tubes were all twisted, one around his ankle, and one around his forearm, which was reaching toward the ceiling and pulling at the source. His face, when it turned to me, reflected his need for oxygen. In its desperation for air his face resembled a flower: eyes and lips were very dark, then like a petal the color faded out until it reached the skin of his ears, which were blanched white.

"Joaquin," I said, "you have to get down. Carefully now, let me help you. Christ, you're going to pull your tubes out." I moved around him, holding up catheters and lines. On the bed, a pile of stars, all as large as the silver one that he was still holding. Some were shiny green, some were red. All the stars had large paper clips pulled through their tops. I could tell he wanted to talk but he couldn't because he was so short of breath. He slowly got down, and within a few minutes I had him in the bed, all untangled, his oxygen tube in place. I sat beside him, the big decorations in my lap.

"What were you thinking?"

"You have to help me," he said. "You have to put them up."

"Joaquin, I have clinic in an hour. I have too much to do before then."

"You don't understand," he said. "My mother and sister are coming in from Puerto Rico today." He paused. Then, he said, as if saying it would make it happen, as if shiny stars had this much power, "They haven't seen me in three years, I don't want them to be scared."

We remembered how to laugh when I was on a chair, my lab coat on his bed, and I was reaching, reaching with each star, hooking it into the air vents and the sprinklers and the porous ceiling tiles. We laughed until every star was hung and we pretended that in their floating shimmer the sight of him, dying in the bed, had been changed. I never saw him alive again, but I always believed that the marvel that happened next was his doing.

That day clinic ran late. Patients who didn't have appointments came in to bring us gifts. I hadn't filled out my lab slips ahead of time because I had been helping Joaquin. When someone was on a clinical trial all bloods had to be FedExed to a central lab. No names could go on the tubes; they all had unique identifiers and specific study weeks and study numbers. Each person had about six tubes and each tube had specific lab requests. I had not prepared any of this paperwork and so when the last person left, I ran with the tubes back to the office. I started spinning and labeling and packing the box, which, when I was done, was large enough to hold a microwave oven. I called for the FedEx pickup and was told I'd just missed the last hazardous materials pickup. I asked for actual locations where I might take the box. They gave me two: one on Fifth Avenue in the thirties and one over on the West Side around Tenth Avenue, in the meatpacking district. I hailed a cab and explained my reason for rushing. The driver did a great job considering the holiday traffic and waited for me when I pulled up in front of the Fifth Avenue store. I ran from the cab with the box and a man was moving toward the door from inside. I thought he was going to open the door for me and so I smiled at him. He smiled back and locked the door. I yelled "Please, please," then said something else, maybe "Fuck," maybe "Fuck you." The cab driver was watching. I got in and started crying. I was so angry. If the blood couldn't get shipped out all these people would have to come back in and have it done again. The cab driver said something so kind I looked at his name. Probhakar, his last name was. We kept the meter going and he took me to the West Side.

The line at this FedEx office extended to the street, but they were open until 11:00 p.m. It was about 9:00 p.m. now. I paid the driver and thanked him for being so kind. The box wasn't heavy but it was awkward, and the line moved slowly, everyone sending their Christmas gifts. People looked happy, rosy. I caught sight of myself in the glass, and I saw myself, but I also saw Joaquin standing on the back of his bed hanging stars. I just wanted to get home. I wanted to lie down. I realized that I didn't have enough money for a cab ride home and was thinking about the best bus route, Tenth Avenue bus maybe to crosstown . . . when the counter opened before me. I smiled. I always try smiling first, but the woman held up her hand to stop me from placing the box on the counter. She saw my red *Hazardous Material* stickers.

"No hazardous materials after ten."

"It's only nine thirty," I said. I could feel the emotion in my voice. I wanted to be businesslike, assertive, but I was anxious and she felt it and was immovable.

"By the time we do all the paperwork the truck will be gone. No."

"I want the manager." A man came, the Christmas mailers were staring and also clicking their tongues. Let's move it, they were all saying to themselves.

"If she said no, it's no," he said, throwing all his weight behind her as the clock moved toward nine forty.

"What is wrong with you people?" I was shouting and I told them everything in a near-hysteria. "All these people will have to have blood drawn again, it is so hard for them . . ." Endlessly the story flowed, and I added that it was Christmas, and they actually started to smirk and then boldly, the woman reached out, not to me, but to the man behind me who was holding a perfectly wrapped something or other in his hands.

The only thing I could do was take the box back to the hospital and store the bloods in the refrigerator in the lab. I'd have to go in the following day, even though I was off, to try and see if the specimens could be salvaged. The dry ice in the box shifted against the Styrofoam and made a sound that I felt in my teeth.

I went outside. Across the street there was an off-duty cab. The door opened. It was Probhakar. He waved me over. "I was worried about how you would get on," he said. He was a mystic, a shaman of goodwill.

"I can't take a cab," I said. "Thanks, I don't have any more money."

"Miss, please get in," he said, and held the door wide open. "Merry

Christmas." He winked. And against the law, we drove to the hospital with the meter off.

"I will wait for you," he said, when I got to the entrance on First Avenue.

"Oh, no, I live just five blocks away."

"You are tired, and I will wait." He sort of bowed his head, his black hair fell forward. He wasn't young, maybe fifty, but he looked . . . tender, I would say.

I was only gone five minutes and when I came down he was there. I was so moved by his kindness, he had undone all the trauma of the evening. I noticed he had a miniature Ganesh dangling from the rearview mirror. At my apartment door, he turned around, "You do good work," he said. "God will bless you." We said good-bye back and forth, the way you do sometimes when you don't really want to leave someone. And although I had not put up a tree, and there were no decorations in my apartment, when I opened the door that night, for just a moment I saw large three-dimensional stars in silver, red, and green hanging from my ceiling. At that moment at least, I was not scared for Joaquin.

Healing

I REMEMBER THE SUNDAY IT HAPPENED. IT WAS IN APRIL and I had decided I would try to clean out my closet. I had a portion of a friend's ashes in a heavy see-through bag. His mother had divided them among a few of us after he died of AIDS-related lymphoma. I was waiting for the right place and time to scatter them, and they were just resting in the cluttered closet on pink towels. I pulled down a box of half-finished poems. It was three in the afternoon, and I opened the box, overwhelmed by all the paper. I said out loud, "When will I ever have time to do this?" And the phone rang. And there was a voice telling me I'd been selected for one of five writing fellowships at the Fine Arts Work Center in Provincetown. I was crying and looked over at the ledge of postcards. Eleven of them had been turned around; Provincetown was the only one remaining address side out. There was Beckett and Yeats and a medieval soldier on a stairwell and a poacher bleeding in a chair with a rabbit at his feet and there was a painting of a pear and Caravaggio's Jesus being taken in the garden. All the beautiful cards I'd selected and suddenly the most beautiful one was just a red stamp with a handwritten date saying *received.* It might as well have said *delivered unto you,* it might as well have said *you will be saved.*

I called everyone in my life, family first, then poets, then other friends. I called Glennon last. Was it possible I would abandon someone again? He wasn't my brother, but I felt the same pull of desertion. Was there a trumpet? The air was broken like that. Miraculously, Glennon told me he was thinking of moving to California, to finally settle down with a man he had been in love with for years and who wasn't afraid of his illness. A man I'd met and approved of.

That Tuesday on my way to work I was smiling at strangers. I felt as though I had finally come out of the dressing room wearing my own skin, and in the mirror I saw the possibilities of my own shape. I was leaving the blue building of death. I was leaving the room with the files in the locked cabinets, each one holding the name of a dead man. I was saved by a packet with fifteen pages of poems and a cover sheet that had my name in the upper right-hand corner. A little packet that had flown on my behalf ahead of me into a different life.

My sister allowed me to move into her apartment in Jersey City so I could save money for the upcoming fellowship year. She lived on the river facing downtown New York City. The view from her terrace was astounding; directly in front of us, the World Trade Center rose every evening in a glass dance of sunset: pink and steel, a parade of people moved seamlessly from the ferry below to their parked cars or to their nearby apartments. My senses were heightened by my happiness, by the smells of the ethnic restaurants, an urban garden: Ethiopian, Italian, Japanese. Was the world this beautiful all along? Where were the men with the plague?

I was just minutes from my parents' apartment and I saw them more than I had for over a year. They were so happy for me, that I would finally have time to write. "You'll be away from all that sadness," my mother said. My sister understood what this meant to me; her own art supplies waited in the room where I was sleeping, waited for her to have her own sacred time. She was going to take care of my car and we decided we would all go up to P-town together for the weekend before my fellowship was to begin.

The only thing I really believe about birth order and siblings is that the child who is new to the family takes the role that is not already taken. My sister had the good role, the smart role, the obedient child.

It was all on her résumé. I came when she was almost five years old. The house was still cooing over her. She radiated contentment and so I howled. She ate what was put in front of her, so I picked and was colicky. She was enraptured with my mother, who had been happy from the moment she was born until just before I was born, when my grandfather died suddenly and my grandmother had a stroke and my mother carried my weight inside her while she tried to care for my grandmother. When I was born I was too small to go home and my mother became septic and hemorrhaged. I cried and cried and forced my mother to turn around and hand me to my father, who wore a navy blue uniform with a badge and a gun and who patiently walked me every night in his shiny black shoes. We split camps. I had dark thoughts and tantrums. My poor sister. How could she be good enough to make my mother happy again?

A few years before my mother died she said to me, "I was depressed after you were born. I couldn't look at you for six months. You were too small to know anything, you didn't care, but one day your sister said to me, 'Mom, how come you never smile anymore?' I decided to snap out of it, for her sake."

I don't believe in blame in families. Our family was, for a short time, a good girl and her mother, a bad girl and her father, and then, miracle of miracles a brother was born and he was a Quaker meeting room. He would be better than all of us, and when he was finally taken from us, his wide, invisible arms were the way we found our way back to one another.

My father, mother, sister, and her boyfriend, Michael, drove me to Cape Cod. I was wondering about all the years when I was sure they didn't love me, didn't even like me. I could feel their happiness about what was happening for me. It was the first step toward the peace that was waiting out there for me, even if it was years away. It was this trip, this pride I felt from them that shifted the earth we were standing on, shifted me back into the circle of the family.

My mother always loved the sea and taught us to love the sea, even after she spent all those hours looking out, thinking it had swallowed her son. Even when, years after that, she spent those moments knowing he had new tumors in his lung before she called him to the beach, called him to come in from the waves and the leaping he was doing in the water. The ocean's waves mirrored our breathing, ceaselessly in and out, unconsciously in and out, and yet within its powerful life, as in our own bodies, death was in every wave. What was beautiful to us was the power of that, though it was easier to say it was the color on the water, or the smell in the air, or the sound, the crashing on the rocks and the echo in the cove that we loved the most. I watched my mother on the first day of my fellowship, her pretty face turned toward the wind coming in with the waves, her pink shirt, her hands, the way she liked to hold them: the fingers of her left hand held firmly in her right fist, a sort of pulling out of herself, a holding on. In her chest, her own heart, damaged by a childhood fever, made its disorganized sound, its chaotic beating that sometimes caused her dizziness or a cough when she tried to lie flat. On that day, facing the wide Cape beach, I imagined her heart was back in its rhythmic pace, for her face was as relaxed as the dune grass and it reflected light the same way. It was a golden day and behind her I could see my father, his quick pace up the beach. He liked to walk fast. He liked people to say he didn't look anywhere near his age. He didn't really, with his still-red hair and thin, quick limbs, unlike my mother who was tiny and gray and who could never walk fast, not with her failing heart and heavy fluid-filled legs. She was peaceful, though, and smiled when she walked, even if it was slow, even when she paused to make the sign of the cross as she passed a church shrine. She and my sister could talk about anything. The love between them was as palpable as an eagle bringing back food to the nest. One carried sustenance, one opened its beak to receive it. There was a seamlessness in their love. Approval. No conflict. A genuine enjoyment between them. My brother re-appeared as a silk thread of unhappiness among us. A thread almost weightless, barely perceptible, but tethered to each of us because it would be unfaithful to let it go permanently. He hovered over all of us, testing our fidelity again and again.

My family left the day I moved into my writing studio. There was a reception that day for the five poets and five fiction writers. In the gallery there was also a reception for the ten visual artists and then a barbecue where we all came together and a picture was taken for the local newspaper. The apartments and painting studios were in a rescued lumberyard just a block and a half from the beach. Stanley Kunitz, one of the founders, welcomed us. I found every time I tried to speak my voice caught in my throat. I was going to be turning forty in a few months and was one of the oldest fellows they'd ever taken. I knew I'd been handed a gift that would alter my life, and I held it in its rosy silk wrapping on my lap.

Once the first welcoming days and nights were past, and little friendships or animosities had begun, the work arrived. I felt more rested than I ever remembered being in my life. My desk faced the window that faced the studios of the visual artists. As I watched them work I learned from them, more than I had ever learned from another writer. They allowed themselves obsessions: one painter did nothing but pods and roots. A huge oil painting took over an entire wall in her studio.

The other thing I learned from the artists was to destroy what was failing. I found it easier just to leave a poem that wasn't working, like abandoning warm-up stretches for the dance. I learned from their physical labor: they carried wood and glass, they carried canvases; hammered cloth to frames. They breathed in chemicals and wore masks, they welded and wore safety glasses. I was at a desk, writing on a computer that even checked its own spelling, lifting white paper into a printer as I sat back and drank juice and watched the artists walk back and forth in front of the juniper tree.

One thing I was not prepared for was the way my identity got up one night early in the fellowship and walked out the back door and over the dunes and disappeared. I felt like a fraud in my little cottage. Even as I read the Penguin classics. Even when I got my acceptance letter from the *Paris Review* in the mail. I was a nurse who had abandoned the plague for seven months and all around me were people, younger than I, who studied literature and writing and worked as editors or had gallery openings. I wondered what I would save for myself when the seven months were over. When the other fellows went back to teaching jobs or publishing jobs I would be left knowing this was all I had ever needed.

I decided I needed to volunteer. I went to the AIDS Support Group, a local enterprise that helped people with disability applications and home care and day-to-day support like delivering meals and walking dogs. I stuffed envelopes, delivered a few meals, and walked two dogs from time to time. I didn't give them very many hours at all, but I felt connected to the town and I felt a subtle link to the real world, which surprisingly, I had some trouble leaving. I didn't know who I would be in the new life. If I wasn't a caretaker, who was I? I wasn't sure I could be happy without the counterweight of suffering.

The writing time was a blessing. The morning opened for thoughts. I woke every day with words in my mouth, delicious as blueberries. I watched the juniper tree change in subtle ways, lose some green, drop a berry, hold snow in its arms, cast a shadow on the cedar wall behind it. The snow piled higher every week. Sometimes I shoveled it, sometimes I threw myself down in it. Always, in those days, underneath all the time passing magically slow, the taste of salt in the air, salt in my hair. Always, my spirit lifted over the hull of a blue boat, lifted and rolled out from under it. More than once I thought that if I died after those seven months I would still have had something most writers never have. The enormity of the gift of time grew each evening, especially when I went to walk the golden lab who was grieving under the bed of his owner. When I leaned under the bed of the dying man and met his eyes the gift was the time to coax this dog out for a walk and some supper. When I sat with the dog on the snow-covered rocks at the seawall and said, "Look at me," the dog did, and I said, "I know," and together we turned and watched the sea pull away under the bright pink setting sun. The gift, the rosy silk wrapping of the time I had been holding in my lap unraveled and spilled forward. I hoped I would never find my way back to the other sadness. In the dunes, the chatter of a bird, the folding over of reeds, whistle of wind. Beside me, grief, disguised as a warm body, licked itself clean.

After the magical seven months, I was awarded a second-year fellowship at the Work Center. The days stretched out before me. They allowed me to meditate on everything I'd seen as a nurse. I remembered all the time I'd spent as a little girl imagining my life as a nurse. Imagining I was Molly Pitcher, lifting parched lips to a sip of water. I realized the years of the AIDS epidemic had helped me live out that vision. With no way to save lives we had resorted to the oldest forms of comforting: a cool rag, a tepid bath, an embrace. Somehow, I understood that those days had healed me. I had seen myself in three dimensions and I didn't dislike what I saw. I also knew that even though I hadn't been able to stay with my brother as he got sicker and sicker, if it had happened now, I would've been strong enough to stay. All the strangers' bedsides had helped me become the person I most wanted to be. It wasn't my identity as a writer that solidified in that second year, it was my identity as a healer.

The Homeless

In the summer of 1997, at the end of my fellowships, I was looking for work. People love to say, "Oh, you're a nurse, you can work anywhere," and that is somewhat true, but it doesn't mean I would want to work anywhere. I wanted to work with people with HIV/AIDS, but by 1997 there were a lot of people who wanted to work in the AIDS field and jobs were at a premium.

On the third Sunday after I was home I saw an ad in the *New York Times* for a nurse/case manager to work in a homeless shelter for men with AIDS. "This is it," I said to my sister. I felt it. I also decided to apply to a low-residency graduate program for my MFA. It helped me feel like I might hold on to a little bit of the peace I found on Cape Cod. I sent my résumé to the address in the *Times* and within a week I got a call for an interview.

The shelter was in the Bowery section of New York City, just above CBGB's bar, a block from Houston Street. It was early July and hot, and I was wearing a summer dress and sandals. The security guard was a good-looking black man with dreadlocks and he told me I could go up. The stairway was dark and smelled of piss. After the third landing a room opened before me. It was a huge loft with circular pillars located throughout the space. There were two small cubicle offices and ten cots with lockers on the right side and ten on the left side. The center area had long tables and folding chairs. Light was filtered by dirty windows that were half open, letting in the honking and occasional sirens from Houston Street.

Kevin came from behind a cubicle. He was a stunning man, dressed in black, with long straight hair and ice-blue eyes. He described the job, which was really three jobs combined: three days working in the shelter doing health referrals, education, facilitating support groups, doing intakes, and helping with benefits applications; one day working as an RN for the drop-in respite area, where homeless men and women came in for breakfast and lunch and showered; and, finally, one day working at the homeless senior citizen site in the park on Delancey Street and making home visits to the Bowery flophouses.

I was used to sparkling clean wards and modern equipment in the cancer hospital, but there was something that made me want that job. It came with a twenty thousand dollar pay cut, but I said, "It's more important that I like my work." When I left after the interview I walked around the corner to First Street and saw TV crews filming an *NYPD Blue* television episode. I took that as a good sign since it reminded me of my father in his uniform when I was a little girl.

At the time I started working at the shelter, I had one true phobia— mice. In every aspect of my life I was always trying to anticipate mice. Someone would say, "You should borrow the cottage in Ireland," and I would ask, "Are there mice? Has anyone ever seen a mouse?" And if their answer was, "Once, in 1964, there was a mouse," I declined the invitation. One afternoon when my mother was very old and very sick and we were sitting on a bench on the boardwalk down on the shore, she told me that she felt guilty about something she did when I was a baby. "You were very little, maybe a year old," she said. "I saw a mouse in the upstairs kitchen, and you were sitting on the only chair. I put you on the floor with the mouse and I stood on the chair." I felt a sense of relief. My phobia now made sense. As a baby I must have sensed her fear. "Don't worry, Mom," I told her. "I would've done the same thing."

Three hours into my first day at the shelter, a mouse ran into my cubicle. I managed not to scream, but I phoned Kevin across the loft as I was holding my legs in the air. He came over and my legs were cramping and he emphasized that there *will be* mice. There were traps. But there would be mice. My heart was pounding. It was very clear to me all of a sudden: I wanted this job and it was a small horrible animal, but it wasn't dangerous, and I could do this, I told myself. I thought about walking out, but decided by the end of the day not to. I held my legs in the air, but once the mouse disappeared behind the file cabinet and was gone for an hour or so, I relaxed. I didn't live here, after all, unlike the twenty men I was beginning to meet with in my little space.

At the shelter, we had people who routinely self-reported that they were HIV infected, or who paid someone to go get a test with their ID, hoping to scam a fake HIV infection. HIV was a way to move more quickly through the public services backlog. More than one person said to me in the course of my work here, "HIV is the best thing that ever happened to me." The shelter system alone was an improvement: twenty beds and a supportive environment as opposed to two thousand people in the Brooklyn Armory shelter, where violence was a common occurrence and no one knew from one day to the next if he would have a bed the next night. City shelters required people to leave in the morning and not return until evening. If someone had AIDS and he was in my shelter, he could come back during the day, and if I agreed he was sick enough, he could lie down. The men locked up their possessions and went unencumbered to a doctor's visit. Not a luxurious life, unless one was homeless.

There was a lot of suspicion about HIV medications, and a big part of my job was to educate the men about the medicines and the choices they had. These were the sons and grandsons of the Tuskegee experiment, in which black men were purposely untreated for syphilis so clinicians could watch what happened as the disease attacked their brains and nervous systems. The long-reaching effect of that travesty was that now another generation of black men was dying. Sometimes, despite illness and falling T cells, I hit a brick wall with them when I talked about medication. Night after night I kept trying, taking the men in one by one and explaining again what the treatment options were and how they worked. I had guest speakers come in, other men of color. I invited some slam poets who were performing pieces about HIV, and gradually some men started the treatments.

Mice continued to come. They managed to eat the peanut butter on the sticky board and not get caught. During one group meeting when we had our chairs in a circle, a family of them came out and got in the circle and danced. There was no other interpretation for it. The men were distracted, and I was freaking, but for a time we all stopped talking and watched the leaping vermin on the warped wood floor. One man in tiny braids said, "This is how the white man keeps us down, he puts us in a shelter with rats and infects us with AIDS so he can kill us." Everyone looked up from the mice to me. "Talk to me after the revolution, Arthur," I said. This got a laugh and a shout of "You tell 'im, sister." We had a truce. Conspiracy theories were put to bed for the night, but as I watched the young black men get sicker and sicker and remembered the gay men dying, my own suspicion of the right wing made its way into me as I drove home each night, passing the poor men on the Bowery, stepping from the shadows for a dime.

Every Thursday I went to my job in the park. The homeless senior citizens lined up before 8:00 a.m. and we let them into the brick building where we served breakfast, lunch, and an afternoon snack. On an average day there would be about a hundred and fifty people using the center. I took the list of the homebound seniors, old men living in flophouses along the Bowery, and went with my escort to start rounds. The flophouse hotels were invisible to the average person walking the city. The entrances, alongside restaurant supply stores or wholesale lighting fixture stores, led up to an enclosed cage. Each building was a little different from others, the tone set by the owner and by the men in the cages. Some flops were only rented to older men, the halls filled with veterans; but some also rented to younger, more violent, mentally ill men.

Before I went to the flops, I thought I knew what poverty was. I thought I was beyond surprise, but I was wrong. I was about to be changed. As I write this, almost ten years later, the flops are gone, sold to developers of the Bowery, the new hot spot for restaurants and poetry readings. When I went there, residents talked anxiously about development. They feared losing the only homes they knew; some of them had lived there for twenty years or more. The flops were long hallways of four-foot-by-ten-foot cubicles, opened at the top, covered with chicken wire. Each floor had one toilet, one shower, and fifty stalls. In the summer the stench of dirty linens and booze and urine and shit was almost unbearable. The men of the flops were a brotherhood of failed marriages, failed jobs. They were reformed drinkers or active drinkers. They were mentally ill or developmentally disabled. Some were really sick: cancer of the throat, leukemia, colon cancer, lung cancer. I tried to do dressing changes in the tiny spaces and my bulk made the job harder. Some men were clean and tried to keep their stalls neat, but they were at the mercy of their neighbors. Roaches filled the door hinges, dropped from the ceiling, ran on the wall behind me, which I was often pressed against. Some men kept Brillo pads shoved in cracks to try and keep the mice from climbing on them while they slept.

In all my years of working I never felt so consistently devastated as during my days in the flops. Every Thursday night I sobbed and swore I would not go back. But by the following Thursday I would get messages the men left with André, the guy who delivered their lunches. And honestly, even though I dreaded the physical space, I wanted to see the men. The men were in a cave with wire walls. The men were in a well, sitting in a bucket, and all along the sides of the well, roaches ran in the dark and dropped into their water. The men found things on the street: a rose-patterned dish, a picture of Italy, a rabbit's foot. Everything they found made a home of the cave and lent it color and mystery. One man with throat cancer found a baby shoe and hung it by its shoelace from his wire ceiling. I was trying to break up pills into powder so he could get them past his big tumor with water. I was smashing the pills in little envelopes to separate the doses. He pointed to the shoe and, holding his hand against the growth on his neck, said, "I looked everywhere for that poor mother. Can you imagine how upset she would've been? To get the baby home and only find one shoe?" I put my hand over his and felt the hard mass pushing into his windpipe, which was why his voice had the rasp and whine of a radiator pipe. He was clammy, and I hoped he would die soon.

There was a man in the flops I called Professor. He was a drinker. Vodka. And a gambling regular at offtrack betting. Even with his addictions he could usually make his Social Security check last for three weeks, but in the fourth week he would be struggling to keep from having DTs and he'd be confined to his stall, where he made sculptures from pennies he found on the street and drew Greek gods on the walls with chalk. In the fourth week of every month he would think about changing his life and get very philosophical about the world. I loved listening to him as he sat on his cot, little tremors in his hands. He had melanoma all over his chest and legs. The skin cancer lesions had been cut out but they didn't heal and there was a putrid odor to his wounds. One day, while he talked about the god Janus, I packed his wounds with clean gauze and covered them with big Band-Aids. Roaches ran across his bed pillow. He picked at little fleas on his chest. I admired him for keeping the penny sculptures. For not dismantling them to buy a piece of bread or a vodka on the rocks. "Smell that," he said, as I took off the worst of the dressings.

"I am dying from the inside out." He had pale thin limbs and a red face with peeling patches on his chin. He had little spectacles, John Lennon glasses we called them. "You are the most stylish man in this building, Professor," I said. The last day I saw him, he took my hand. "I wish you were my daughter," he said. I hugged him good-bye, despite the fleas, despite the wounds. If I had a big house at the sea I would've put him on a bus with ten of the other men and taken them out of there. They would worry about leaving their little homes with the wire coverings, with the hanging baby shoe and pictures of Rome. It doesn't matter. They are all dead now. In place of their stalls, a coffee bar or luxury lofts with thin metallic lights. I couldn't be the Professor's daughter, but I was someone's daughter. I had a glimpse of what I would be asked to give and I hoped I was learning enough to be able to care for my father when the time came.

It was impossible to work with the homeless and hate my apartment, no matter how small or inconvenient it was. I came home and was grateful for shelter, especially on very cold nights. I lived in Jersey City in an apartment building across from my parents' building, but the place was very small, and my sister, Cathy, who lived in the same building, also paid a lot of money for a tiny apartment. We realized that if we pooled our resources we could easily rent a better place in downtown Jersey City, near the ferries and the PATH train. We looked one Saturday and Cathy immediately wrote a check for a large three-bedroom in a renovated warehouse across from a working matzo factory. The whole neighborhood smelled delicious, like burnt toast. The best part was the view. From both the terrace and my bedroom window we had a clear view of the World Trade Center on the New York side and the back of the Colgate clock on the Jersey side. The Colgate clock was, I believe, the largest clock in the world, with the exception maybe of Big Ben. We had resident-only permit parking on the street, which saved almost three hundred dollars a month. I was accepted into a low-residency MFA program in Asheville, North Carolina. I would travel there twice a year for two weeks each time, so I could continue to work on the Bowery.

Soon after we moved into the big new place, my sister got assigned to Ottawa, Canada. She was a technical banking consultant with a company based in California, and she was hoping, after a year in Canada, to be assigned to the New York office. I suddenly had a massive apartment to myself except for every other weekend, when my sister flew home. My parents moved down to the shore after being evicted, along with eleven other senior citizens, from their apartment building, which was converted into condominiums. We settled into a routine where I went down to the shore on the weekends. I would go to the boardwalk with my mother, whose heart was starting to fail.

In the days of working with the homeless, I found myself comforted by the fidelity of words and painted them in gray clouds on the white walls of my apartment: *history, sleep, release.* I invited poets to the shelter and the men proudly displayed their voices. I loved the familiarity of the Bowery. During this time, my mother's heart failure worsened. My sister tried to come home as much as possible, but by default, I wound up spending more and more time with my mother, something that would later convince me that nothing happens by accident.

I Come Home to My Mother

MY MOTHER WAS A PINK BUD FALLEN ON THE GRASS IN THE orchard. My mother was the green light in beach glass, and the ornate reliquary on the front of the Book of Psalms. She was etched in wrinkles from years in the sun, and delicate in her frame. If she was a musical note, she would be the plaintive A-flat. All the little arguments of my youth—my dress was too long, my hair too wild—all the criticisms disappeared. Not just eased, but vanished. My mother and I entered a new rhythm. I arrived on Friday night. She cooked something I liked. On Saturday we did errands. My father rested after a week of doing most of the chores on his own, since the stairs were getting more difficult for my mother. Sometimes when we did errands she waited in the car, but more often we just moved very slowly together from one point to the next. Sometimes I held her soft, soft hand. When we were younger we used to laugh about the Polish women in the neighborhood who walked hand in hand. Now I took hers and said, "Let's be Polish." It gave us permission to hold one another, because even though it was just hands, we were, after all, embracing. I drove back on Sunday to the big apartment with the great view. At sunset, the World Trade Center held all the colors of the sky, held the reflection of the clouds and the reflection, too, of the Hudson River between us. The guts of the Colgate clock enlarged like a spiderweb across the grass, and the big hands reminded me that this time with my mother was passing.

When the heart fails slowly it takes the breath and holds the fluid, so that the ankles and legs swell up and cramp. My mother had a lot of pain that she never talked about, but it got harder and harder for her to sleep. She lost her appetite because the fluid was also in her liver and her belly swelled and limited her hunger. She didn't sleep well because when she lay down the fluid rose in her lungs and made it harder to breathe. She found that the couch was easier for her. My sister and I now took turns sleeping on the recliner in the living room. My mother said we were a big comfort; just being in the room had a calming effect, she said. For us too, we wanted to say. We both feared, and loved, the curved sight of her getting smaller on the couch.

I worried about Cathy because all her life, while I was finding ways to argue with my mother, she was talking to her and sitting by her side and gaining her approval by working hard and having good taste in clothes and occasionally placing a bet on the numbers or going to Atlantic City. My mother and sister loved good clothes and patent leather heels and shiny bags. I worried about her losing so much time with my mother, being in Ottawa on assignment in what was more and more likely to be my mother's last year on earth.

But this, for me, is the marvel. My sister's absence allowed me to sit with my mother facing the ocean while she told me all the things I'd always wanted to hear. Her absence allowed us to hold hands and taste the salty sea air. We wore sweaters in autumn on the nearly deserted boardwalk. Crashing, curling water of a final year. Rocky, seaweed, black rock year. Year of my poor father, jumping up to reassure her he would not die before her. Look at how young he still was, he was leaping down to the laundry room and running back up the stairs with everything folded and clean. He was vacuuming, she needn't worry, he was fine, she would be taken care of. My mother continued to cut his oranges into little triangles of juicy orange light and to serve them in a white bowl and to thank him for all he had done, but she still somehow worried, what if he died? What if she was left? She prayed about this, unrolling the elastic band of her prayer book whose spine was split from holding the bulk of holy cards from all the people who died before her. She undid the elastic band every evening while he ate his oranges and murmured his gratitude, and she prayed for all of us, while her bulging ankles cramped and pulled against her. While her white hair curled in wisps from her face.

I prepared to begin the low-residency MFA program in Asheville. It was September 1998. I was to start in January. My parents were thrilled. A low-residency program meant that twice a year, in January and in June, I had to be on campus in Asheville. If you missed the ten-day residency you had to skip the entire semester. My parents seemed to understand suddenly, after all these years, how much writing was tied to happiness for me. They saw some of the sadness I carried as a nurse and understood how language balanced the sadness with joy. They wanted me to get my degree; they wanted to see me in a different life.

My parents liked to come to my poetry readings. My father would go outside venues afterward, to smoke a cigarette and work the crowd sub rosa, a holdover from days on the vice squad. He acted like a random member of the audience and casually asked the other smokers, "What did you think about that one girl? That nurse?" He would tell me later everything they said, good and bad. He didn't believe in a false sense of confidence. He had trouble with the *I'm OK, you're OK* movement. "What? Is EVERYBODY supposed to have self-esteem?" he asked. "Look, this kid can't even read, but he feels good about himself."

My mother was getting sicker and my boss allowed me the freedom to take a day or a half day so I could go with her and my father to her medical appointments. In mid-October I went with them to my mother's cardiologist. The doctor was a beautiful Catholic Filipina, and she understood my mother's fear of all medical procedures. At this visit she talked frankly about the condition of my mother's heart, about the hopelessness of her situation, but also offered a few extreme measures, which my mother declined. My mother wanted me there. They both wanted me there, a kind of witness to this decision not to go forward. My mother's face was remarkably unafraid. I knew it was her faith that let her sit calmly in the chair across from the doctor. My poor father, whom I could barely stand to look at, was in the waiting room, getting free pens from drug reps.

My mother asked about making it to Thanksgiving. The doctor was not hopeful, but reiterated that it was all a guess, that she could only estimate the time remaining. We left the office. It was a perfect October day. "Oh, Red," my mother said. "I just want to live a little longer." Then, after a beat, she added, "Give me a cigarette, will you?" We all laughed, and she smoked, and they got in their car to go back to the shore, and I drove into Manhattan and went to my office, where the people had been lining up, looking for something from me that I was hesitant to give.

My sister was in Ottawa and we talked almost every day, and she talked to my parents almost every day. We decided that everything was worse for my mother because their apartment was up a steep flight of stairs. They had a chance at a bigger ground-floor apartment in the same complex, and we all talked about it, and they decided to take it. They couldn't move in until December fifteenth, but that was fine, it needed work, and my mother wanted to buy a new rug. Thanksgiving was at my aunt's house, and we all knew it was my mother's last Thanksgiving. Secret gamblers, we collected money from all the guests for our annual pool. Everyone got to pick one time for when they thought the turkey's button would pop. The previous year I was the judge and my father won, which raised everyone's suspicions that I was in cahoots with him, so this year my sister would monitor the cash and the turkey.

My mother sat next to my father on the couch. She was wearing a blue sweater with a single strand of pearls. He watched her and kept his arm over her shoulders. All their years together, heavy in the air. The years were a Celtic knot, the absence of my brother was a cross, their skin was luscious with loss, but sweet with the taste of their years together. I didn't know what he would do without her. She made a statement. "I really want to live until Christmas," she said.

My sister and I decided to do Christmas. My mother and father would come stay with us for a few days before Christmas. My mother was made happy by our spending time together. After months and months of having to walk the steeps stairs to their second-floor apartment, my parents were finally going to be able to move into the apartment downstairs. The apartment was vacant because someone had died, the unspeakable knowledge of their apartment complex at the Jersey shore, where retirees gathered and lived out their days. My parents were preparing to move on December eighteenth. On the twelfth of that month we went to a carpet sale at Macy's. My mother was very out of breath and she walked so slowly down the aisles that people bumped into her. I tried to shield her, but people were clicking their tongues at us and pushing past. We found a pretty rug with pale pink roses and a mint green border. She almost collapsed onto a pile of rugs rolled up near the cash register. It could be delivered in five days. She would have it for Christmas. She looked up at me. I wanted to hold her in my arms there in the department store with the hanging displays of dramatic rugs. The man was impatient with her and her slow, uneven signature. Everyone seemed to be begrudging her this final pleasure, this last new purchase; they were all too busy to enjoy it like we were. Couldn't they see that the flesh around her legs was so wide it was weeping?

My mother lived until Christmas. She got to spend one night in the new ground-floor apartment with the pretty new rug. Then she came to our house and my sister and I let her do little things to help with the preparation: unwrap ornaments for the tree, slice carrots down the middle. A handful of relatives also came, but for us it was about the last Christmas with my mother. She had clearly been holding on for this and her body was changing slowly: her wrists grew bonier and her nose was a bluish color and slightly larger from lack of oxygen. Her fingers were clubbed, but she still painted the nails a festive red. My father seemed unnerved to be away from their new apartment, from their old things, and he found our apartment cold—the modern concrete walls held in the chill.

Still, by Christmas Day we were really revved up. My mother wore a soft pink cashmere sweater and winter-white pants. She wore pearls. Her feet barely fit in her shoes and so we helped her raise them to the ottoman and we handed her a white wine. We truly enjoyed the day, that was how it has always been with my parents; they just wanted to be with us. We asked them to stay for a few days after Christmas. My mother could barely hide her happiness as my father struggled to hide his frustration about not going home, but for her sake, he agreed.

On December twenty-eighth they headed back to the shore, and later that same day my father called to say my mother was short of breath, more short of breath than usual, and she was scared. Dr. Luna suggested he bring her back up to the hospital. We agreed to meet there in an hour. It was possible now that she would die. She had one other goal, to live until January third and make their fiftieth wedding anniversary. We imagined we might have asked for too much. She was given Thanksgiving and the bonus of Christmas and it was cold and she didn't do well in the cold. Her poor heart. Her poor wet legs. Her cold toes and clubbed fingers. She took her prayer book and a scapular and a rosary with her to the hospital. She took Saint Jude oil and a pale pink nightgown. I could barely stand to imagine her packing these things. Did she direct my father to pack them? Did she turn to look at the new rug, still in the process of opening flat against the floor? Her dishes were not yet unpacked, but a black-and-white photo of my brother was at an angle on her dresser so that it seemed as though he was looking at you when you entered and left the room. I am sure she turned to look at him as she left, her breath nearly gone. She was comforted by him as she rested her hand on her chest, which was struggling against the fluid building and building, pushing her to the deadline she had escaped twice already.

Here is a cliché I believe in: what goes around, comes around. Nearly thirteen years earlier I had worked nights for less than a year in the emergency room of the hospital where my mother was heading. There was a nurse in the coronary care unit who was a new graduate at the time and I routinely did her the favor of keeping cardiacs in the ER overnight so she could get a handle on the unit, then right before the morning I would bring the patients upstairs. I would carry out all the orders first and help stabilize the patient. It was a nice thing to do and the nurse never forgot. When my mother was admitted all those years later, this nurse was still on nights, and now she was in charge. She made a private place in one of the coronary care unit rooms and dismissed the visiting-hour restrictions for us. No twenty-minute restrictions, no restrictions at all. The kindness I showed her years earlier paid off in spades.

My mother's body was leaving her and she wasn't afraid. My mother was leaving us, and we didn't want to be afraid. In fact, we'd imagined we might not be, but we were; the monitors measured her heartbeat, measured her blood pressure, but there was nothing to measure the gap that was widening between us. We were holding her hand as though across a crevasse. Light was splitting a rock between us, was splitting the earth.

My mother lived for two days. The first night I slept in the room with her. I fell asleep with my head on her knee. She was sleeping herself. At some point she awoke and rubbed my head and I heard her say, "You're such a good girl." It was as though I'd been in a cage in a jungle and someone had slipped a key in a banana leaf to me. I undid the rusty lock of the vision of myself and I went wildly into the trees. There were colorful birds and ripe fruits falling around me. I pretended I was still asleep so the words might hang between us in the air for a little longer.

In the morning I went home to sleep and my sister and father spent time at her side. My father said the chaplain had come in, and my mother liked him. He was a big redhead. He blessed her. She talked about her children. I went back to the hospital in the afternoon. My mother started talking about me going to school. I was supposed to leave on Saturday, which was only three days away. She said, "No matter what, promise me you'll go to school." I promised her, but told my father and sister that I would not leave her here like this. She knew this, I think, and she got more and more agitated. In the middle of the second night the nurses noticed she was unconscious and called us. My father, my sister, and I spent the rest of the next day by her side, although she didn't wake, not even when we were stroking her hand and talking to her. Not even when my father leaned over and lied to her, saying, "We made fifty years, Margie, you can relax," which made my sister and me both cry.

Finally, at three thirty in the afternoon the monitors reflected the absence we were seeing in her face, which was open and calmly turned toward my brother. My father turned to me and said, "That was a gift from your mother, now go to school." I didn't cry but I did call my aunt and headed to the elevators with my father and sister and suddenly, from the bottom of my soul, vomited in the hall bathroom.

My father insisted I skip the funeral and go to school. I would be able to go to one night of the wake, but not the funeral Mass. I was torn and it was late. The next day we were supposed to go to McLaughlin's funeral home to pick out holy cards and order a casket and bring my mother's clothes. We decided on the pink cashmere with the white

pants and the simple pearls. I was in my room, still unsure about what
to do, though I had called Delta and checked on my flight, checked
on my rental car. My father entered the room, in delicate blue light
from the skyline. He said, "I've been thinking about what I would
say if anyone is STUPID ENOUGH to say something about your
not being at the funeral." There was a pause, and he added, "And I
would tell them, you could've done the easy thing and stayed, but you
decided to do the harder thing, and honor your mother's wishes." He
had freed me suddenly, completely, to go to Asheville. He was always
trying to find a way to free me.

At the wake my mother was a bird in a box. My mother was a beautiful, falling bird, her rosaries like prisms in her hand. I slid a sand
dollar into her pants pocket and rested my hand along her hip bone,
impossibly hard for someone so *gone*. I could feel her head, just days
earlier, resting on my left breast as she was sliding down into the bed.
It was Christmas Day and I was handing her a glass of wine. It was
Thanksgiving Day and she was throwing her arms around me; she
was in her blue sweater, and her arms were so heavy to lift she had to
use her shoulders to throw them. The arms were clumsy, they hit me
in the face, they were around me. It was a beautiful day in October
and we were leaving the doctor's office and she was saying, "I just
want to live a little longer."

I landed in Asheville on the day of her funeral, which was the day
before their fiftieth wedding anniversary, and it was snowing. I took
the rental car, and because it wasn't heavy snow yet, I drove along the
Blue Ridge Parkway until I reached a closed road in the mountain
and spent the two hours or so I knew was the funeral time reading Seamus Heaney's sonnets to his mother. I also offered prayers
of thanks to the young boys with cancer who taught me how to be

with the dying, and to Gene, who lost his face to a boat propeller, for teaching me to look unflinchingly at what frightened me, and to the homeless men for showing me how portable a home is, how I might take my home, take my mother in a car over a pass in the snow as if it was where we'd always lived. As if a home was a mountain.

The first night of school there was a dance in a big barn. We circled with glasses of white wine and red wine and talked about poetry and why we were there. I told a few people about my mother and then went back to my room, which was in an old dorm on a hill, and climbed into the bed. Was it possible to be this happy on the day my mother was buried?

I Come Home to My Father

AFTER MY MOTHER DIED I FOUND IT HARD TO WALK UP the four flights to the shelter. Cathy and I went to the shore every weekend to see my father. Sometimes one of us went down, sometimes both of us. He stayed in their new apartment on the ground floor and he bought two single beds for the guest room and put them side by side. He bought identical end tables, identical lamps, and a little rose-print rug. It was a room for children, and we were his.

We knew his weeks were long and he started to prepare for our coming on Thursday. We tried to leave him cooked meals in the freezer, and once a week my aunt invited him over. He went to the public course to golf alone and met one or two other old men, who took to him; my father was good with people. Still, I tried not to think about how long his days were in those first few months. Cathy and her boyfriend took him to Ireland that April. They met cousins and went to the town where my grandmother was born and stood in the church where she was baptized. He walked to a bookstore in Dublin, where he bought me everything he could find by Ciaran Carson, a poet whom I had said I liked once. I couldn't be in Ireland with them because I would need all my vacation for the second residency in Asheville in July. I tried not to envy my sister this time with him. I tried to remember how lucky I was to be with my mother on the boardwalk.

I cannot remember a patient from those days. I was fine all day until I was driving home. In the long line to enter the Holland Tunnel, I would remember my mother was gone and imagine my father alone at the shore. I would cry in my car. My friend Rachel in Chicago told me once that she cried all the time in the car on her commute home. She said there was something about the car's cocoon and the pace of moving from one place in life, like work to another place, that tore at people's souls. There was no escaping one's thoughts in traffic. Rachel cried about the broad expanse of Indiana, of the farm she lived on when her mother left. Sometimes she remembered her childhood hunger when she was driving home planning a meal. "Watch the other drivers," she said. And I did. Everyone seemed to be weeping.

Six months after my mother died I was down at the shore visiting my father. I would be heading back to school in two days. I was trying to sleep in the little bed when I heard my father moving around the apartment. I got up. He was short of breath and his pulse was very fast, very faint. I wanted him to go to the hospital, but he didn't want to go because the next day my sister was coming down and a girl who was on their Ireland trip was coming over. He wanted to have this little visit, he had been preparing for it. For the next couple of hours I sat up with him. He was in a recliner and I was in a big chair by the window. Between us the couch stretched out its cushions and the history of my mother's shape against them.

The next day I watched my father. I was trying to count the pulsing in his neck, and his breath was catching when he talked. Finally his visitor left, and I was cleaning up sandwich plates and my sister was washing dishes. My father said, "I think I should go to the hospital now." I was very good in those situations. Efficient. Calm. We drove his car to the Jersey Shore Emergency Room, where he registered and leaned over the desk and was somewhat dusky in color, so he was whisked to a bed. He got a little oxygen and an x-ray and some medicines and fell asleep, already more comfortable. The ER doctor was a beautiful Indian man with a lilting, musical voice, and he included me in his plans for my father. He put the chest x-ray up on the light box in the room where my father was sleeping and pointed to a white circle in the lung at the same time I put my finger on it and said, "That's a tumor." I knew what a tumor looked like from all my years at the cancer center, and he nodded and was very gentle in his manner. "I will admit him and have a cardiologist see him," he said. "But I think the problem with his heart is from the tumor pressing on it, crowding his chest." My father slept, his red hair fanning out on his pillow. I called my sister and told her he was going to be admitted. The white spot, the baseball in his lung, was still unconfirmed.

The cardiologist was young and unreasonable and denied that there was a tumor on the x-ray. My father woke up while I was arguing with him. "It's fluid," the cardiologist said.

"It's too dense for fluid." I was shaking my head at his stupidity.

"We'll repeat the x-ray tomorrow and I'll let you know."

My father said, "Don't fight with him, Mare, he knows." I was put out. And unconvinced, and wished we had the Indian man for his doctor, the gentle voice and casual touch on my father's arm. My sister arrived and decided she would work from home. "You have to go to school," she said. It was exactly six months since I'd first gone to Asheville; I was starting my second semester. The next day I was on the road. The cardiologist told my sister that the repeat x-ray was fine. I was relieved, but suspicious, deep down imagining the worst.

The campus was beautiful in July: magnolias and cows, high grass and singing insects. Thunderstorms and checkered tablecloths. I met my new adviser and he had read one of my favorite books: Hans Zinsser's *Rats, Lice and History.* What, we wondered, were the odds of that? I told him about my father, and I also told him about my mother, and we hunkered down under a big oak to write out my reading list and to figure out my work for the next six months. He called me "sister." He reminded me of why I wanted to live in a world where the names of flowers were as important as the names of gods.

My father was much better, according to my sister, who generously had used all her vacation time to stay with him. The medicine slowed and strengthened his heart, and freed some trapped fluid. I had to accept that I might've been wrong about the tumor. I turned to the cows, to their heavy eyes, and asked them to let him stay with us forever.

My sister has an amazing gift. She can paint, make prints, and do pastels and watercolors, but somehow, even though she was the child with all the promise, she hasn't found a way to have a life that is about making art. I wanted this for her, but instead, it was happening again, she was at my father's side, and I was in the Blue Ridge Mountains, eating vegetarian plates in the politically correct cafeteria and talking about how to tell a story in a poem.

Although most of the time I would break up the drive of fifteen and a half hours into two days, I left very early on the last day and tried to make it home. My father was discharged from the hospital. It was a Sunday, so if I could get there, my sister would fly back to Canada on Monday morning.

I held the steering wheel very tight all the way and when I got to the New Jersey Turnpike I had to pull off for a few minutes and sleep. My father always used to say, "No one is pulling the plug on me. I want everything done, no matter what." I would say, "Then make Cathy your proxy because I am a big plug puller." Despite all those talks he made me his proxy for medical concerns and my sister the banking and life insurance person. He had such a streak of fairness in him, even in those days, he was making sure we were treated equally.

After another two hours on the road, in the dark, I reached the tollbooth exit. I tried to hand the attendant my ticket and money but my hand cramped in a claw around it. "You have to pull it!" I said, in pain and with some urgency. She was a large black woman with salt-and-pepper hair, and she eyed me suspiciously. Was I toying with her? She reached out, though, and felt the cramp pull back. She tugged and the ticket came free with the five-dollar bill, which almost ripped in half. I reached across the wheel with my other hand to take the change, then shoved the painful left hand under my thigh. I drove like that until I reached my father's apartment. My hand slowly unfolded. I must've gripped the wheel too tight for too many hours. I told my father about it, built the story up a bit, added some dramatic details. "Yeah, that happens to everybody," he said. Does it? Oh. I believed him completely, even though over the next six years as I told the story, I always asked, "Did that ever happen to you?" And people would stare back. "Never," they'd inevitably say.

My teacher for the second semester was Steve Orlen. Once the ten-day residency was over we were expected to write to each other every three weeks. I sent poems and annotations, and he wrote back. It was the pattern of the program, but when I got my first response from him, I was unprepared for his generous offering. I opened the envelope casually, but by the time I finished reading his comments I was sobbing. I wanted to go to school because I wanted a degree, but I realized now I was actually getting an education. I was getting a wise package in a Priority Mail box. I was learning to be a better poet.

After the first packet, I opened all the other packets more carefully. I poured a glass of wine, undressed, and got into bed to read them. I was completely vulnerable to his comments about poetry, which were meticulous and reverent. Steve expressed some concern about my ability to do the essay semester, which was my next semester. He thought my annotations needed work, needed to be fleshed out a bit. I studied as hard as I could, and read everything I planned on reading and more, but he still had some doubts.

At work, the patients were coming and going. It seemed as though my co-workers were always fighting. We had to have a psychiatrist come in once a month to help us keep the peace. It was hard enough to have to look after the men.

Most of my life I have had pain in my right hip. My mother told me that when I was born the doctor said, "There's something not right about that hip." They saved their money and took me to a specialist, who said everything was OK. As I got older it would make a painful snap and feel like it was coming out of the socket. Sometimes I limped without realizing it, and when I would complain, my mother would say, "You and that hip! There's nothing wrong with it, we took you to a specialist!" I took to chewing aspirin in high school and for the most part kept quiet about the pain. My mother hated that I chewed aspirin. "It's a sign of insanity," she said. "That guy in the Stephen King book chewed aspirin—the writer in *The Shining.*"

In the year after my mother died, it got so bad that even when I was driving I would have tremendous pain that sometimes made me break out in a sweat. I decided to go to a doctor, who told me it was a back problem and sent me for physical therapy. The doctor said I had mild arthritis and nothing else. The physical therapy helped a little because I think I had done something to my back from favoring my hip, but I still had the snapping sounds and I still had the pain. My friend Wendy said, "Back pain is always about anger." She sent me photocopied articles on rage and posture. And of course, everyone said I should lose weight. When I sat with patients in those days I would feel completely disconnected from them. I would nod and smile and take the papers they needed help with, or go over housing programs with them, or medicines they needed, but I was concentrating on the burning pain in my hip and resenting them for not doing more to help themselves. I had been given a beeper but never turned it on, and never gave anyone the number. I slid it to the back of the drawer and kept it turned off. I wasn't paid to be on call. Another nurse, Donna, who had become a friend, answered her beeper even on the weekends, even when she was at the mall with her children. I looked at Donna and saw the saint I used to be.

My father offered to have Thanksgiving that year, the first year without my mother, and my sister and I went about inviting family to the shore. My father was enthusiastic and we all pitched in, my sister doing most of the cooking and preparation, which she insisted she loved. The day went well, a perfect mixture of laughter and sadness. It was a gorgeous day at the shore. The last of the red leaves covered the ground outside the apartment. My father had made friends with a young couple upstairs who had a new baby boy, and they stopped in. My father held the baby on his lap. He beamed at the little round head and lifted him in the air. My father could always make babies smile at him, none were ever afraid. I could picture myself now before I had memory, in his arms like that, giggling in the same effusive way. Before the meal my father said a prayer for everyone present and "Margie and all the other absent family: Johnny and Kit and Mike and Annie." We were surprised when he invoked my mother and grandparents and my brother. Their names settled among us, our eyes half-raised to one another, focused instead on the pale turnips in the gold-banded bowl.

It was the Sunday after Thanksgiving, and my sister and I had been at my father's apartment since Wednesday night.

"You'll miss us," I said.

"I will," he answered, "and there's not a damn thing I can do about it."

"You could move in with us." My sister gasped. My father heard her. I shouldn't have said anything without talking to her, but how could I not ask him? He was so lonely. My father dropped the subject and my sister and I said we wanted to drive down to see the ocean. I apologized and she was calm about it. We talked it over. We went back and laid it out for him.

"Dad," I said, "take some time to think about this. You can let us know in a week."

"Mare, I don't need to think about it, I'd go right now."

So few times in your life can you sit in the pleasure of such a moment, knowing you have done exactly the right thing, the one and only thing that will free you from regrets later. The three of us sat in the energy of that day, with my mother's appreciation and approval hanging over us in the room.

We made a list of all the furniture. We had too much between us. My father talked about the couch in his apartment. "I can't stop seeing your mother there," he said. Everything I owned fit in my bedroom, so it was really about my father and my sister, and she decided he should not have to lose one other thing, which was so in character. She offered to put her furniture in storage. We told my aunt and uncle, who lived very close to my father. My sister and I heard some relief in their voices. We imagined they felt a little worried by his presence. My aunt offered a meal once a week. Everyone wondered what he did with his time. In any event, we were going to take him away. We were going to bring him home.

The night before I was leaving to drive back to school for the winter residency I went down to the shore to help with some packing. My sister had arranged the movers for the day I came back in two weeks. At one in the morning I got up to go to the bathroom and my father was sitting in the recliner in the living room.

"What's wrong?" I asked him.

"Nothing, Mare. Just a little uncomfortable." I checked his pulse, it was wildly racing.

"We are going to the hospital," I said.

"You are going to school," he said.

"I know, I know." I couldn't believe this was happening again.

We went to the emergency room, where they did an EKG and a chest x-ray. He was on a cot facing the center core. I was standing beside him. I looked at the x-ray film they hung on the white box light.

"I hope that's not yours," I said.

"Why?"

"Because the tumor that that moron said was fluid is so big now it's obliterating the lung."

"Jeez, Mare, pretend to have some good news, why don't you?" But he looked at me. We knew. We'd known all along.

A week later my sister and I moved most of our furniture into a storage space and turned our den into a third bedroom. Our building had all the practical conveniences we needed for my father, secure parking and an elevator. Once all my father's furniture was arranged, he reasserted himself as head of the household, and within days, it was as if we were living with him. This was a good arrangement, and we played along. He held on to his dignity and my mother's couch.

The next day I headed out on schedule for the long drive to Asheville. We agreed I'd call from school. The drive down was its own special meditation. I love a long drive, the music, carefully chosen, like a sound track for the trip. I took the slightly longer route, through the Blue Ridge Mountains, and made the first day a short one, since I'd been awake most of the night. I stopped in Lexington, Virginia, and from my room in the Ramada Inn, I saw horses walking in a field. I saw the full moon on their backs, which dipped down. I saw two heads together in the grass, and understood that I was not surprised to find we would be losing my father sooner rather than later.

I woke early in the room above the horses and hit the road by 7:00 a.m. On my drive, I thought about my life since my brother had died. I wondered whether all the bodies that somehow felt connected to me were placed there so I would know how to handle this now. To let go of the one person I have tethered myself to all my life. I remembered what my mother said about me as a baby, how difficult I was, how unsatisfied, how she spent the first six months in her bed, depressed, watching from under the rim of the candlewick bedspread as my father lifted me to him with one hand, loosened the billy club on his belt with the other, and with his patrol cap tilted back, walked me in the halls until I settled against him. As I went on to do my whole life.

Now after a lifetime of holding the hands of the dead, and advocating for their pain relief, and attending to their bodies after their breath was gone, now I would be asked to attend the hardest loss of all. In World War II, my father had been missing for ten days. He carried a wounded crewmate for ten days after their plane was shot down. We had a telegram that had been sent to his mother declaring him missing and a subsequent letter preparing his mother for the inevitable loss. He is *presumed dead,* the letter said. As a child I was fascinated by his miraculous reappearance into the world. Although it was long before I was born, I imagined what it must have been like for my grandmother and mother when he came walking from where he was lost into the clearing and back into their lives. Now, so many years later, I was being asked to walk with him in the woods in Germany, to smell the ham in the bicycle basket, the ham he stole on day seven to keep himself alive. I wanted to be with him when he ran zigzag in the woods, when the blackbird perched above called out a warning. I wanted to save him from soldiers who might, at any moment, burst from the woods and shoot him down. I would stand in the woods with him even if I knew there was no way he could be saved this time.

Some friends asked me why I didn't just take a leave of absence from school. I explained that I wanted to, but that my father, who took so many years accepting the part of myself that was sustained by language, had developed an urgency about my finishing school. I think he felt he was ensuring my happiness somehow if he knew I would complete my graduate degree. This was my essay semester, which meant I had to produce a critical paper of roughly fifty pages and ongoing packets of poems. I decided to research the use of the sacred in meditative narrative poetry and to use Brigit Pegeen Kelly's poem "Song" and Seamus Heaney's long poem "Station Island." As usual, the faculty matched me perfectly with a teacher named Daniel Tobin. Dan was Irish, a former theology student from Harvard. I told him at our first meeting that I should probably have taken a leave this semester, but explained how I started school missing my mother's funeral and how now, even though my father had just been diagnosed with advanced lung cancer, he insisted I attend. "I will do my best," I told him, but I was worried about being able to make it work while we cared for my father, and I was also working full-time. Dan was understanding and we agreed just to plod ahead and tackle the problem of a leave if the need arose. Then he asked what I liked to read, and I said, "Nothing before Yeats." "OK," he said, "then let's start with John Donne." I liked him already; he was going to be a ball buster, like McClatchy, and I was gearing up for the challenge.

He was determined I get the essay done, and while I worked in the homeless shelter all week, commuting into New York, I used the evenings to do my reading. On the weekends I set up my father's breakfast and began typing. Sometimes after six hours at the computer I came out of my room, opened a soda, and sat down.

"Are you finished with that paper?" my father asked me one day.
"No," I said. "Of course not."
"Why are you sitting down then? Get to it."

I cursed him under my breath as I headed back into the bedroom, but in this way, I had every packet in on time, and better than that, my father offered to read the essay and gave me suggestions on clarity and point of view. We wound up talking about religion. We spent many afternoons going over symbolism and faith. It was one of those miracles I'd come to believe in, the serendipitous kind, when everything in the universe lined up, and even though my father was dying, we were talking about belief, and his was strong. We were talking about justice and peace of mind. We were talking about tragedy and the lessons of tragedy, and he was weeping from time to time. The cop, the rock, the head of vice, decided at last to let me in, and it was as wonderful as I'd always imagined it would be.

At least every other weekend my sister flew home from Canada. The minute she arrived I collapsed into my bed. We developed a good working rhythm of the house, of getting groceries and preparing meals, and sometimes my sister took extra days so she could go to my father's chemotherapy appointments with him, and I did the same, so he never had to be alone, or with a stranger. We were fortunate in that our lives allowed this. On the Bowery it seemed all the old men were gradually being evicted, or when they died, their stalls stood empty. Everything was being demolished or developed, and as I drove home on Houston Street I looked down toward the Bowery and imagined the men in their disappearing stalls. So many of them were men like my father: veterans, tough Irishmen who liked to drink, but somehow, we were allowed to have a different life, we were saved from their despair. Or maybe we had saved one another. I was going home to my father with a tongue sandwich from Katz's Deli. I was going home to watch *The Sopranos* with him. I was going home to spend some of the few remaining days of his life with him, with the tumor that was a melon in his chest wall.

We counted our luck like this, day in and day out, in the big apartment facing the New York skyline. I got so comfortable with death in a room that it rose, like the shadow of a coatrack behind the door; it rose, like an orange moon over a field illuminating the scarecrow. Or death was a tornado crashing into a school yard in upstate New York, killing nine kindergarten children in a cafeteria.

"Can you imagine?" I said to my father as we watched the news report.

"They're in kindergarten!" he said. "They'll be fine."

Then the news anchor added that a team of psychologists would be at the school when it reopened to help the children cope.

"That's that," my father said. "They'll be talking about this for the rest of their lives."

When I was more than halfway through my essay and my father was more than halfway through his chemotherapy, he fell. It was one in the morning and he had some trouble waking me up. When I finally heard him he had crawled to my room. The apartment was bone cold. For an hour and a half I tried to lift him. He wasn't heavy but it was awkward and my right hip was throbbing and everything I once knew in the hospital about helping people up vanished the instant I saw my father, frail, in his pajamas on the floor.

"Just leave me here," he said.

"What? I can't leave you on the floor!" I called the police, asked for someone to come help me get him up.

"We have to dispatch an ambulance," the woman said.

And they came, two strapping twentysomethings, and they raised him in the air like the feather he was. My father was cheerful, he liked meeting new people. "No, I'm fine," he told them, and tucked in once again, under the big comforter, he fell asleep. I signed all sorts of releases with the ambulance drivers to keep them from taking him to the hospital. The following day was a chemotherapy day, but I couldn't imagine him getting more medicine, he was already so weak. I remembered all the conversations when he said he didn't want anyone pulling the plug, and I was wondering if I would have to address that sort of situation anytime soon. He didn't get his treatment that Monday. His blood count was too low, and he got a shot of something to raise it. We also stopped by the surgical supply store and I got a walker and a urinal. We had a talk about his fall while I made him some fruit and oatmeal at home. I wanted to get an attendant in the apartment for when I was at work.

"Forget it, honey," he said. "I don't want some stranger sitting here talking about themselves, watching a soap opera. I want to be left in peace."

I had expected this answer, and my sister and I had discussed it. "Well," I said, "you need to know what we are talking about. You could fall right after I leave for work and lie on the floor for twelve hours, pissing on yourself, or you could die alone, or I could have to come home and find you dead. Is that what you prefer to a stranger in the house?"

He loved straight talk, my father. "You got it, Mare," he said. So every morning after the fall, I left the apartment and said a prayer that none of those things would happen.

On May 2 I sent in my final version of the essay. My father read it and gave his blessing. Daniel Tobin gave his blessing, and now it had to go to a second independent reader, who would either accept it or reject it. Every semester there were rumors about people who were told they needed to repeat the essay semester. It dawned on me that all the work of the past five months could be rejected. I tried not to think about it. I tried not to think about my job. I tried to focus on my father, and my father's body, and how the tumor was returning to its original size and could be seen through the open neck of his pajama top.

One day I came home from work and asked about his day. "It was good," he said. "I watched them paint lines in the new parking lot." Another day he said, "See that plastic bag caught on the power line, Mare? I've been watching that bag all day." He was too tired to read, but he was always watching, it was what he did. He was on a kind of stakeout all by himself, no partner, patiently observing.

While I waited for a decision on my essay I went on a binge of rereading my favorite books. *Jude the Obscure*, *The Plague*, *The Odyssey*. The stories seemed especially dark. It was almost summer, and my father was a bird living with us. His feet were knobby and blue, his legs had shrapnel scars, and he was talking and talking about the war, and about how he fell from the plane. He told cop stories and stories of the shoe factory. He told stories about being a boy and seeing his father killed by a hit-and-run driver. I was absorbed in each tale. Each moment that he was talking and I was listening made an arc of space in the room that was not big enough to contain the way we were together. I was my father, I was falling from the plane. He was so tired, and drugged on Ambien, but he wouldn't lie down. I was so exhausted I was collapsing, so I said, "Forgive me, Dad," and I pushed him gently back into the bed. He fell back, his legs, still bent at the knees, rose up. He let out a low "Whoa" and I rolled him on his side, where he fell instantly asleep. It was his last summer, and there were only a few days remaining for us. That night, I eased him into sleep and covered him with blankets. I saw myself in him. I was not afraid for him. I was not afraid.

When my sister came that weekend, he wanted to talk with her alone. Whenever he wanted to be alone with her he would say, "The smoking lamp is lit." They would smoke together while I stayed in my room. Some nights I rested my head on the windowsill and watched the lights of the World Financial Center and the World Trade Center.

I loved the copper domes of the Financial Center's buildings, their femininity brought balance to the skyline. At the base of the copper-domed buildings, the ferries to Jersey City and Hoboken would glide back and forth across the water.

One night the *QE II* came down the Hudson, and it was so large the river beneath it disappeared; it looked like its own city squeezing between us. My father had a wool throw across his knees and I lifted his feet to my lap so I could cut his toenails. My sister and her boyfriend were sitting on the couch. My father said, "Mare, no matter what, I will be at your graduation." I told him I knew that, but he said again, "No matter what, do you understand?" Oh God, my father was planning his postdeath visitations already. "I know," I said, and unintentionally snipped off a piece of his toe. The foot on my lap pulled back and the blood was plentiful and dramatic. My sister flinched and my father shouted "Jesus Christ!" and eventually, once I'd repaired the damage, we were all laughing.

My sister and her boyfriend by now had been together for thirty-two years. Longer than most marriages. He is Italian but we tease him about wanting to be Irish. My sister and I sometimes talk about why they never had children. Neither of us fully understands our decision not to have our own sons or daughters, but we imagine it is connected to seeing the great wrenching loss of Johnny's death in our parents' faces, in the soft curve of their bones. Now her boyfriend also cares for his parents, who are in their nineties. He shows them the same affection he has always shown us. In those days when we were losing my father, Michael's presence was electric. He picked up meals, he helped clean up, he made us laugh by imitating characters from *The Sopranos*. He bent toward my father, delicately. Was it possible my father would have a son beside him as he died after all?

The following Sunday my sister was home, packing for a flight to Canada the next day, and my father complained of a headache. I could see the tumor at his clavicle. I noticed that his face and neck were swollen. He was nauseous and his left arm was tight with fluid. I told my sister I was worried he had superior vena cava syndrome, a potentially fatal complication of cancer when the tumor blocks the blood flow from the upper body and causes brain swelling and compression on the chest and heart. He told me later that night that he didn't think he could stand the chemotherapy the next day; in fact, he didn't want it anymore at all. I said I would go to the doctor's office in the morning and explain his symptoms. I didn't tell him yet what I thought it meant.

The doctor was about my age and very tender, and as soon as I described what was happening, he said, "It's superior vena cava syndrome. It will be fast now, probably this week." He suggested we get hospice in so my father could be pronounced at home without having to be taken to the hospital. He gave me prescriptions of liquid morphine and suppositories for nausea. We lived in a rough neighborhood and many drugstores limited the amount of narcotics they kept on hand. I had to try three pharmacies before I found one that could fill the prescriptions. Once I had the medicine in hand I started driving home and I realized I was about to do the hardest thing I ever have had to do in my life. I loved my father's freckles, his red, red hair, his beautiful hands, and I would be holding them and telling him he was going to die. My sister had stayed home another day to see what the doctor would say and when she opened the door I just said, "I can't talk," and moved closer to him and she followed and I knelt next to his bed, and said it exactly like the doctor said it, because he said it perfectly.

I saw my sister take the news like I did. She straightened her back. I told my father about the morphine. "You don't need to have pain," I said. He looked at me. He seemed quite serious, but there was a glint of the old challenger in his eyes. "I don't want to be too sleepy," he said. "I want to see how I handle it." Then he paused, "And I want to see how you handle it." He laughed and reached into his bedside drawer and handed my sister a wad of cash. "Let's have Italian tonight," he said. "And for Christ's sake, get some good wine." He called my aunt. "Looks like I'll be checking out this week, Fran, if you want to come for a visit." I took the phone from him and explained and she agreed she'd come up from the shore the next day. We called a few of his friends, who also made plans to stop by, and my mother's older sister. My father decided this would be another adventure, and he was smiling, and he was breaking our hearts.

The last week with my father remains one of the happiest of my life. He told us how proud he was of both of us. We talked about his life and my mother's life. We ate really good food. We drank wine, and when his friends Pudgie and Claire came they talked about high school and my mother and CYO basketball. They talked about the day my father and Pudgie went and signed up for the Army Air Corps and headed off to World War II. My father talked about Graham Greene and John le Carré. He took one more opportunity to remind me I was to finish school. Two days before he died I got a letter saying that my essay had been accepted by the second reader. He was happy reading the complimentary review of the second reader. I made a point of saying I couldn't have done it without him.

We didn't really talk about his death. We knew it was happening, but there was no fear in the room. We asked death to wait in the high-back chair. We filled the blue vase with calla lilies and gave death a cup of coffee. We offered it a thin mint, but being death, it didn't know how to appreciate it. We did, though, those of us still living. We chilled the mints and had them after lasagna, after our nightly dose of wine. The liquid morphine sat, like holy water, next to the statue of Saint Jude. All was going according to plan. What were the odds? To be blessed at my mother's bedside, to be blessed at my father's.

On the last day my father was a little agitated. He'd made his peace, he'd had a few laughs. Midday I offered him a little morphine to go with his glass of red wine. He took it. It calmed him a bit.

"Mommy will help you," I said. I repeated this a few times over the next hour or two. My sister held one hand, I held the other. From time to time, we gave him a drop of morphine, like a drop of sea air. Finally I said my mother would help him once too often and he stirred and looked at me. He was aggravated. "Jeez, when!?" he asked, and as was my habit over all those years of feeling like an authority on death, I glanced around the room, then said, quite assuredly, "In fifteen minutes." It was unlikely, but true, that roughly fifteen minutes later, he looked between my sister and me, at the space between us but farther away, almost at the door, and said, "Jeez, there she is," and smiled and relaxed back into his body. His eyes closed. He wasn't dead, but he was leaving. I told my sister to drop his hand, as I did, fearing he might feel pulled back from whatever was happening, and she did. He continued to go somewhere that we had to call a coma because we were so inadequate in understanding the miraculous. He lingered another ten hours, but he never woke. He barely stirred. He was so quiet in his death that it was when we were turning him, my sister and I, that we noticed it had happened. He exited like your breath exits when you rise from the ocean, abruptly, with the confidence of another to come.

We waited a few minutes and then called the hospice nurse, who was a mere fifteen minutes away. We called McLaughlin's Funeral Home. And then we sat with him. And then we sat with each other. My sister and I. Between us the spirit of our father and mother and brother, and how could it be that later we would admit we were both sitting there feeling, of all things, lucky?

As if to punctuate one of the stories my father liked to tell, the funeral workers, when they came, were dressed like thugs. There was no other word for it. They were in maroon velour sweat suits. They looked like bookies from Secaucus. They had a red rubber stretcher with no sheet on it. What the fuck was wrong with these men? My father was a war hero, a retired police captain. I lost my mind. I was screaming at them and they were blankly staring. They were placing me in some category in their mind, in the "Crazy, disturbed family" category, when all along it was about their bad clothes and their disrespect. I made them take our sheet, and then I cried like I have only done two other times in my life.

When we picked out his casket the next day, we bought one with a secret drawer where we put my brother's ring and my father's final gift from my mother—his cherished first edition of John le Carré's *The Spy Who Came in from the Cold*.

The Beautiful Unbroken

I FELT SOMETHING SHIFT IN MY BODY AFTER MY FATHER died. It was knowledge. It had the heft of a loaf of bread when it settled in my gut and offered me sustenance against the grief. I had begun my life with the dream of a few women: Kateri Tekakwitha, Clara Barton, Molly Pitcher. I saw myself in a painting and I was cradling the head of a suffering man or woman. Now I was middle-aged and I had finally fulfilled the dream. I wasn't a saint, but I had been blessed to meet so many who were suffering that the body had finally delivered all the lessons it held.

I thought of myself during the time of my brother's illness and wished I could have another chance to care for him. I learned how to be there for him from Jack, the boy who had testicular cancer, and from Tony the baker, who surrendered to his leukemia. I had learned all the gestures that a suffering person needs. I practiced daily like a musician and my hands learned how to move over the suffering body unconsciously.

Nursing was changing. It was inevitable. We became scientists and technicians, theorists and surveillance officers. We prepared for catastrophic emergencies and were funded generously by bioterrorism. Modern hospital wards had machines beeping and clicking their alarms. Tubes and iron bed rails segregated the patients. I got a job working from home as the New York regional coordinator for The Johns Hopkins Bloomberg School of Public Health. I studied research data, wrote reports, and didn't miss, for one moment, the suffering men.

After my parents died, I was grateful for the people to whom I had ministered. When I thought of them, I thought of them turned on their backs. I imagined their feet in basins of water. I saw their tremulous hands, picking at the bedsheets. I felt their hot fevers, their cracked lips. I was their honored guest. I remembered Bernard, and saw his family in their home movie slides. I put out my hands, and they rested on Frank's fresh tar burns in the room in New Mexico. I saw the healing circles of his bright pink flesh. I saw Gene in Georgia, fresh from the boat accident, his sliced face and the delicate blue sutures that held his skin in place over his empty eye socket. I remembered holding his hand in the dim room. And I remembered all the men with AIDS: Peter over the zoo, Gernot in the tunnel, Joaquin standing, tangled in his tubes, hanging Christmas stars. I put my head on my arms and thought of Howard's suicide and how I had held my head on my arms the same way on the day he died. I could see the bathroom with the African violets. I remembered the men in the flops, their odors and their despair. I wanted to thank all of them. It was their bodies and their invitation that enabled me to be with my parents when they died. It was the sacred time with strangers that helped me understand how necessary it was to be with my family. I traveled and sought answers and eventually found my way home. The way home was lined with those whom I barely knew who had allowed me to stand next to them when they exited their bodies and sent their souls flying around the room and out the window.

Bowl of apples. Gorgeous September day. A Range Rover pulls into the parking lot below my window. Orderly life of newspaper delivery, of pink quilted robe and coffee slipping away as my sister says, "Mare, they're saying a plane hit the World Trade Center." I pulled up my shade and saw smoke billowing out from the tower. All the while, in those minutes, below my window, men and women were parking to walk to the ferry or the PATH train, all the while people slowed, the world was slowing down. News was coming through the TV and people's cell phones were ringing. I leaned on my windowsill because it was still my room.

The well-dressed men below stopped by their cars. I saw the second plane; it came out over the river where it turned and seemed to angle up toward the place in Tower Two where the glass made a line around the building, like a sash. It headed for the ribbon of glass. The men below my window were transfixed and placed apart from each other as in an architectural model, so when the plane—I can't say hit, it didn't *hit,* but when the plane flew *through* the glass, some of the men sat on the ground next to matches and pigeon shit. Sat, in their good clothes, in pigeon shit, and one I remember, put his head in his hands.

The beautiful day became the backdrop for a stunning fireball, which was, truth be told, an amazing color. I wore a pink quilted robe. It was all I had except for my arms on my window ledge and the men on the ground below my window. They looked so alone. Didn't they want to be held by one another?

The day disappeared into the "Oh my God" that was coming from all the mouths of the transfixed people. I was a coward at my window, and I vomited against it when the first Tower fell. The collapse of the second tower was just about death, the Pentagon was hit, planes were still in the sky. The turnpike was closed to all traffic except for ambulances that were flying toward us from all over the East Coast, flying in a line of sirens, under a quiet Newark airport. All day I was thanking God my parents were dead so they didn't have to see what was happening.

In the end, all my grief was for the death in me. I had to look in the mirror day after day knowing that despite a life of wanting to be a saint, of wanting to be a nurse-detective, of wanting to be a hero; a life of watching *Rescue 911* on TV and seeing myself racing into the river or crawling into the burning car, I had done nothing. I did nothing for days on end. I never even walked the two blocks to the area where the ferry carried back the burned men and women, the commuters in shock. I saw in the mirror a pink robe, I saw a pale girl who was cutting away the outline of her skin. I was stepping out of the story I starred in and getting into bed, where for the first time, moonlight kept me awake, moonlight that was usually blocked by the towers. The dead meanwhile settled in the air as a fine white powder, settled in apartments on the New York side, settled in air vents and on tea cozies. *Settled* is the wrong word: the dead blocked the vents, tasted like metal in our mouths. From my bed, I listened to the fighter jets make their circles over the harbor and saw, as if for the first time, the Towers evanesce.

Every day, when my sister went to work, she left the *New York Times* open to pages and pages of obituaries, to pictures of the missing. I had my own private service, which had no flag, no candles. It was a map, a Rand McNally map of the United States, and I carried it from room to room, looking for a new place to live. My sister said, "I will never move from here." Everyone was standing together, reclaiming the city, reclaiming their lives, but I (failed heroine in the biggest story of my life) was preparing to run like hell.

I grieved the person I did not become. I buried the ideal, and when I did, all anxiety left my life. There was no one left to disappoint. I was so ashamed of what I discovered on the day of the planes that I could barely stand to hear about people serving soup to firefighters, or giving them massages in between their shifts that never seemed to end. When the police officers and firefighters mentioned that their feet burned through the soles of their shoes within minutes of standing on the smoldering rebar, someone set up a tent to soak their feet. When their breathing suffered under the metal smoke, someone opened a tent for breathing treatments. A friend who lived a few blocks away welcomed Baptist cleaning crews from the South, who came on a bus from Georgia to clean apartments near Ground Zero. Every night on television, the faces of the new heroes. I was in my robe, working from home. I answered the door for the FedEx man who brought me work I could do at home, and examined the map for a new life.

I decided on Missoula, Montana. The country in the weeks following the attacks made a show of itself. There was an air of camaraderie. I was reminded of a few lines from "The Plague Victims" by Marcel Pagnol. In that story he wrote:

> "In 1720, as you know, Marseilles was devastated by the plague. I congratulate myself on not having been there at the time."
> "Please also accept our congratulations on your absence," I said.
> "And we must congratulate ourselves as well," said Yves.
> "But the people of Marseilles," said Monsieur Sylvain, "had no such cause for congratulation."

This was how it was after September 11, 2001. All over the nation people were congratulating themselves on their patriotism. Barns were painted as flags, cars were painted, the flags were huge or small or flying from antennas. Money was falling from the sky, but in the city, the bad taste in the air could not be undone by a flag; small candles could not make a path through fire, which burned until after Christmas. In New York, people had no such cause for congratulation. The dead were not even in the shape of themselves. There was a clearing center under the thousand screaming seagulls of Kill Van Kull, where men in hazmat suits looked for a bone chip, looked for an eye.

Montana. I said the word all day. I told friends. I told the colleagues who were sending my work to me. My neighborhood filled with moving vans. So many businesses in downtown New York had to relocate that this once perfect location, these streets near the ferry, were suddenly filled with exiles. For Rent signs were everywhere, yet by September 13, every square inch of commercial space had been rented in downtown Jersey City, even in buildings yet to be built, so the prices for apartments stayed sky high, despite the exodus. There was no doubt among the landlords that renters would be back in numbers larger than ever.

I mailed my résumé to Montana and called my friend Rachel in Chicago. "This is crazy," I said, "but you're the only one I can ask. Would you want to drive with me, in the winter, to Montana, and then pay your own airfare back to Chicago?" To this day, I remember the beat, it was a second or less, it was a musical note, a bird's quick chirp. There was no silence in the beat, and then she said, "I'm there."

Even AAA advised against the route I had planned across the country through wintry North Dakota to Montana. "But you're Triple A!" I said. "You should be supportive!" I couldn't be persuaded otherwise. The trip west was a hand-stitched red wallet, a fantasy pouch chock full o' cash in my back pocket. Rachel's husband, Pat, also offered to come, so he and I split the driving while Rachel sat sideways in the backseat eating red string licorice. Pat carried all our luggage in and out of motels. The trip took five days, and in North Dakota, our nose hairs froze between exiting the motel lobby and the car. We had a quilt covered with hearts and a green reindeer. We had rosary beads and a magnetic Saint Christopher. I carried some clothes, a few CDs, and all my poetry books. I shipped my bed and a writing table and a dresser my father refinished. My belongings were too few to be moved by themselves, they said. I would have to be *bundled*. I liked the word and imagined my life in a blanket tucked in the back of a Mayflower van riding through the snow. This would be my new life. My parents were in a leather satchel, their names and dates on holy cards: Saint Joseph, and Jesus as a Child with a Lamb. One was my mother. One was my father. The car was a ship as we floated west. There was snow ahead of us and snow behind us, but where we were, it was never snowing. It was as though the gods had made a path and it was brilliantly reflecting the feathers of birds, it had the blue of ice in it. We sang songs, *more miles than money,* we sang, leaping from our skins into the icy air.

By the time we reached eastern Montana I had space. No glass. The September fireball only occasionally wakened. Maybe once a week I saw the falling day. And then, a hawk took a duck. Talons speared white, and they skimmed, the hawk and the duck, body-heavy, together, across the hood of my car. A spot of red grew on the duck's feathery belly, and the duck's wings: inadequate, clumsy, blocked my view for just a moment, suspended there, so that for hours I remembered the claw, and the call, and the blood.

Forty-eight hours after arriving in Missoula, I had a job and an apartment. Pat and Rachel flew back to Chicago. My apartment had a small porch embedded into the substantial limbs of two maples. It was a tree house. I unpacked. I played the September Eleventh movie over and over in my mind. There was a claw-foot tub. Missoula was an Easter lily, I could feel myself rising.

I worked in a community health center and I forgot that there would be so many people who still needed help, who lined up like it was the first day of a holiday sale. Please go away, I wanted to say. On the twenty-fifth day of May, when the maples were all in green and the porch was fully shaded, high winds and hail hit the house. Then the sun exploded out and there were sixty or more hail balls on the black slat porch, some lying on leaves that had fallen in the high wind. I loved the unexpected chaos of bad weather. I loved shelter and the smell of ice in sun.

On the first really warm day in July, I called in sick and went to Seeley Lake. The water was a green baptism. The cold lake was a velvety confessional. I fell on my knees and asked forgiveness for the desire to abandon all the people who needed me. The bones in my back challenged me: "Who will you be if you aren't helping people?" The lake answered, as it always did, with its bath of forgiveness, its silky acceptance. I took the answer to be this: "You will be a floating girl, who can be held up by the dark, sandy bottom of a lake."

The romance of the lake held just long enough, just until I had to stop on the road for a lumbering cow, just until I heard a siren come over the hill, until I heard the sound of a child falling away. I packed my beach towel. The next day I would go back to work.

A couple of nights later, the poet Sandra Alcosser called me at home. Mutual friends had said we'd like each other. We had a long talk and made a date to meet. It was the way it sometimes is with poets, our ideas were tripping over each other. She and I talked about September 11, about caretaking, about poetry and how it descended from its place above the maples and held me in the room over the leaves. Right before we hung up, I almost said, "I love you," but I stopped myself.

Instead, when we met four days later at Bernice's Bakery I blurted it out and said how it shocked me, my impulse to say it. She was laughing and nodding, she was saying that was how poets were when they found what they needed. A bird picked at apple Danish crumbs that fell from our laps. I saw young boys on inner tubes racing down the swollen Clark Fork River. I thought of my brother and imagined he was well and racing in this new town with the violet light. There he goes, I thought to myself, as the river carried the laughing bodies away. I no longer needed him to forgive me. I no longer needed the image of Molly Pitcher, or the sacrifice of Kateri Tekakwitha. I felt completely connected to my life. A cobalt-blue butterfly was my new life, hail balls on a green leaf, a hundred coots bobbing on the lake, the parchment blossoms of an elm tree blowing outside my window like a scene from a Kurosawa movie. The new life loosened the muscles around my chest. My breath eased, my bags lightened. I turned back from the river. Flowers were white cups holding the dead.

Exactly one year to the day, on September 11, 2002, I woke in a hotel room in Helena. I was there for a statewide HIV/AIDS meeting. I put on a silky gray blouse and a silver pin that depicted the fable of the fox and the grapes. I left for the meeting a few minutes early so I could get gas. As I filled the tank, a man about my age, fit, with jeans and a snap cowboy shirt, looked over.

"Your tires look really low," he said.

I am not cut out for the pioneer life. "But are they *flat?*" I asked.

"No, just really low. I'll check the pressure for you." He bent down, circling the car. Each tire was only half of what it should have been.

"Well, thanks," I told him. "I'll get it later." I was thinking I'd get someone to help me later, I was not fiddling with hoses in my good gray blouse. But he just took over, walked around the car, pulled the air hose, and filled them in minutes.

"Can I buy you breakfast?" I was ashamed at my laziness, at my hesitation to get dirty, but he was smiling like we were old friends.

"No, thanks," he said. "I'm driving my father to Glacier Park. He's eighty-eight and he's dying. We live in Texas and he's never seen Glacier. Come, I'll introduce you."

I said my name and he said his. We shook hands and I followed him to the cab of a black Suburban. His father was a wisp of a man in the passenger seat. He tipped his cap, he was laughing at his son's ability to meet someone while he was stopping for gas. "He makes new friends everywhere," he said. He was proud of his son. He was looking past me. Will Glacier Park be soon? Will it be worth it?

I told him he would be amazed at Glacier Park and suggested a place to pull over, a place he would most likely see mountain goats. We all said good-bye and I headed off to my meeting. I decided I would take September 11 back from the terrorists. This would be my new story for that day. A single story of one death, the journey of a father and son, the thoughtful gesture of pumping air into a stranger's tires. I gave up the planes to the sky. I gave the fireball over to the lake. I gave the falling bodies over to the falling leaves. I gave the fear, the vomiting, the failure, over to snow, which comes every day all winter long, until the soul is wiped clean.

I have found it, I thought, as week after week I entered the Mission Mountains, as I entered the freezing lake with the unexpected lily pads. I lost my parents, and then two towers fell, and it was the same grief: too large for anything I had ever known, but not, as it turns out, too large for Montana in winter. The fox leaping in snow carried them away from me, the endless falling of ice flakes as big as quarters. Inestimable value of snowfall as money, jingling in my pocket. I found immensity and it opened the tightness in my ribs, loosened muscles in my chest, until one day, quite unexpectedly, my breathing resumed. It was effortless, this breath of happiness.

The precious find was also the domain of language; poetry shaped the new life, words in the turret room below Mount Sentinel rose with the moon behind the antique barn windows with etched designs. Windows that didn't open, that held the sun in summer and the cold in winter. Windows that let in stinkbugs and ladybugs and box elder bugs, but also let in words, like warm huckleberries in my mouth. Peace came in around the molding and settled in my spine, and loosened in my hips in the pool at the women's club.

In February 2004, I was awarded the Amy Lowell Traveling Poetry Scholarship, which meant I would be paid for a year to leave the continent. I could go anywhere. It was amazing to me that once I found my way home to my parents, and then after the terrorist attacks, found a new home in Montana, that I was being told to leave again. I decided on Ireland, on the place where my mother and father learned to endure my brother's loss.

In September 2005 I began my fellowship in Ireland. In Ireland, stone crosses were the conscience of the living and they shot up in fields where sheep huddled in rain. I started unpacking the faces and the bodies and the stories I had carried for thirty years. They were as luscious as fruit in a wood bowl rubbed with salt.

I lived in Tramore, in an apartment facing the sea. Sea or mountain, it didn't matter, the beautiful unbroken entered me, and so everywhere I was, the dead were leaving, peacefully, in single file. I dedicated an entire day to the Professor from the flops. Each day, I released a death, and each day I took in a living thing: a horse in the fog, a rabbit in the grass. In this way, balance returned to my joints, my hip slid back into place so that I could actually walk hills in the freezing rain, and almost keep up with the old men and women of the town, everyone out, rain or shine, to stand on the Doneraile Walk and look at the sea. The beautiful unbroken was the balance. The beautiful unbroken was the invisible line between the living and the dead. It was finding a way to be with them without sadness. I held my parents in a small pack on my back and took them to the sea, because they loved the sea. I understood completely the gift nursing had bestowed on me. Caretaking had made the home portable; everywhere I went there would be someone who would need a kindness, and I would try to attend them.

When the time came to leave Ireland I found I was leaving another home. My cousins Andy and Kathleen, the neighbors, the librarians, the heavy butterflies, as heavy as almonds, the salt on my tongue, the crosses, the pillars in the skeletons of churches, the round tower at Ardmore, the men outside the bookmaker's office, the women in pink foam curlers talking at their gates. I left having shifted into something like profound happiness, a prolonged peace buzzed in my brain, like the cicadas. At last, a steady thrum of happiness had entered me.

Acknowledgments

I am deeply grateful to my agent, Bill Contardi, of Brandt and Hochman Literary Agents, for his wisdom, support, and guidance. The team at Graywolf Press has been a writer's dream; a special thanks to Katie Dublinski for her meticulous editing. A writer needs little more than time and space. For the gift of time, I would like to thank the Fine Arts Work Center in Provincetown and the Amy Lowell Poetry Traveling Scholarship. For my apartment on the Irish Sea, I am grateful to my cousin, Andy Taylor. A special thank-you to Karen Rowland and Casey Plunkett for their lovely cottage in New Zealand, and to Sophie, Elise, and darling Finn who read to me at night.

I am humbled and grateful to the patients who allowed me to be an honored guest at their bedsides. I thank them, and their families.

Finally, to all my other friends and supporters—thank you. You know who you are.

Bread Loaf and the Bakeless Prizes

The Katharine Bakeless Nason Literary Publication Prizes were established in 1995 to expand the Bread Loaf Writers' Conference's commitment to the support of emerging writers. Endowed by the LZ Francis Foundation, the prizes commemorate Middlebury College patron Katharine Bakeless Nason and launch the publication career of a poet, fiction writer, and a creative nonfiction writer annually. Winning manuscripts are chosen in an open national competition by a distinguished judge in each genre. Winners are published by Graywolf Press.

2010 JUDGES

Arthur Sze
Poetry

Robert Boswell
Fiction

Jane Brox
Creative Nonfiction

MARY JANE NEALON is the winner of the 2010 Katharine Bakeless Nason Prize for creative nonfiction, selected by Jane Brox and awarded by the Middlebury College Bread Loaf Writers' Conference. She is the author of two collections of poetry, *Immaculate Fuel* and *Rogue Apostle*. Nealon lives in Missoula, Montana.

The text of *Beautiful Unbroken* is set in Adobe Garamond Pro, drawn by Robert Slimbach and based on type cut by Claude Garamond in the sixteenth century. This book was designed by Ann Sudmeier. Composition by BookMobile Design and Publishing Services, Minneapolis, Minnesota. Manufactured by Versa Press on acid-free 30 percent postconsumer wastepaper.